Revolution in Training

THEODORE B. DOLMATCH

ELIZABETH MARTING

ROBERT E. FINLEY

Editors

Revolution in Training

Programed Instruction
In Industry

AMERICAN MANAGEMENT ASSOCIATION
1515 BROADWAY, TIMES SQUARE
NEW YORK 36, NEW YORK

This is No. 72 in the AMA
Management Report series.

REVOLUTION

IN TRAINING:

Programed Instruction

In Industry

AN **AMA** MANAGEMENT REPORT

Contents

ACCENT ON THE MACHINE

Introduction

A recent visitor from the Southwest Pacific declares that, for him, the most impressive characteristic of American industry is its *human* resources. It is not our wealth or our machines, he says. "We are slowly getting some money and we can get the machines, but we are just beginning to realize that the men who run these machines must have so many things that our workers don't. Things you in America take for granted: technological skill, a familiarity with machinery, and an ability to 'understand' the tools that you use."

By now, the American ability to develop and get the most out of machinery has become legendary. It is the product of our growing up in an industrial milieu, and it creates in us a never-ending need to develop still newer machines and newer techniques. These inevitably are more complex than the machines and techniques they replace, and they in turn demand even newer skills and knowledge as they are improved upon. This circular process was one of the original roots of American industrial success, and it has become characteristic of our society. It helps to produce the ever-growing goods and services that we are so proud of. However, it forces us continuously to extend our knowledge and abilities. In fact, to sustain the physical world we live in as it becomes increasingly complex, it is more and more vital that our mental horizons be widened accordingly.

If we need still additional motives for insuring that our human skills develop at an even greater rate, we can point to the intensified competition we face from other countries. Our machines can be copied, and our sources of new materials are increasingly available to other nations. If we are to continue our growth and stay competitive, we must do so through our knowledge and our capacity for further innovation.

A related incentive, of course, is the competition we face from other ideologies. Material wealth is not sufficient to guarantee our success in this important struggle. We must use our "human" wealth in this battle too, and our victory depends on our minds and spirit even more than it does on our machines.

But why belabor this point? The lines are clearly drawn. We must develop the capacity to handle our complex machines just as we must develop our capacity to handle complex ideas. This is why we are so concerned now with education, both industrial and academic. This is why we search for *new ways* to learn—because we have so many *new things* to learn and so many *old things* which we must learn better.

AN ORGANIZED, SYSTEMATIC APPROACH

Our search for new ways to learn is the basis for our interest in programed instruction. Here is a new method of learning, based on research into the learning process itself. It is an extension of our facility for invention, of our desire to do things more and more efficiently. Programed instruction is an approach that has come out of the laboratory. It now remains for us to put it to use.

Essentially, programed instruction is an organized, systematic approach to teaching. It derives from experiments and studies in learning behavior.

In the 1920's, Professor S. L. Pressey, of Ohio State University, began his pioneering work in this area. His efforts, unfortunately, received little attention. However, in the early 1950's, the pace of development accelerated tremendously, owing largely to the studies of Dr. B. F. Skinner, of Harvard University, and Dr. Norman Crowder.

Programed instruction tries to get the learner to participate actively in the learning process. It presents the information to be learned in small steps, each one designed to build on those preceding it and each one easily comprehended. The order of these bits of information is precisely formulated; it is the product of tests and retests which insure that the development is clear and remains clear to the learner. This precise design and the student's involvement in the material help to reinforce learning and continuously motivate him to go on.

RELEVANCE TO INDUSTRIAL TRAINING

A great deal has already been written about the use of this instructional technique in schools and colleges. Programed instruction is now being used to teach English composition and trigonometry, spelling and algebra, statistics and logic, languages and music. On the basis of experience with these courses, it would seem that programed instruction offers certain specific advantages. Some of these, research indicates, may be particularly relevant to the industrial training situation which is the sole concern of this book.

The complex work that goes into developing a program can be compared with the work that precedes a job analysis. Just as the job analysis attempts to produce consistent job performance, so a program should produce consistent terminal behavior. This means that we now stand a better chance of getting consistent training at all our decentralized locations. Branch office and plant personnel can have the benefit of the same material that is used at headquarters. Thus the variables of instructor personality, ability, and perception of what is important become less of a problem.

The built-in motivation supplied by programed instruction should improve the rate of completions in a given course or program of training. We know how many starters we have, and, alas, how many drop-outs. Since programed instruction permits the trainee to proceed at his own pace, with constant feedback and reinforcement, the resultant security should be important in reducing the numbers of those who give up too soon, who too easily permit themselves to be distracted or prematurely intimidated by the work they see before them.

Other advantages and some of the disadvantages of programed instruction are described in this volume. However, *only time and your own experience will provide answers that are completely satisfactory to you.*

A TOOL, NOT A PANACEA

The prognosis is good, but one caution is very necessary. Our need for trained personnel is so great that we grasp eagerly at any device that promises assistance. Yet programed instruction is not a home remedy. The construction of a program is a sophisticated process, and the quality of the courses which use its principles and methods is directly related to the quality of the people who prepare the necessary materials. Intelligence is a basic requirement of all programers, but it is not enough: special skills and knowledge are required. These are obtainable, but they are not the haphazard result of training in subject matter, psychology, education, or writing. Programed instruction is a new discipline, and we should be prepared to pay the cost of developing proficiency in it.

Yes, programed instruction is a new discipline. It is, however, not a panacea, not a replacement for all the other training techniques that industry has developed. Rather, it is one more tool for us to use as we develop our skills and extend our knowledge. It will be helpful in many industrial training situations, and it will be worthless in others. It will be better than some of the training we now provide; it will also be worse than some of it.

Here, then, is a revolutionary development that commands our attention. It has been called "the most important development in education since the invention of the book," but it is significant even if it is only the second most important, or the third. And it is a revolution in training which has great significance for industry and deserves to be adapted to industry's needs. In this book, we attempt to show how this process of adaptation is already taking place and to suggest how programed instruction can help training managers in a wide variety of businesses to meet their ever-increasing responsibilities.

—THE EDITORS

Hard-headed management is not to be stampeded into innovation simply in the name of "progress." Any new technique, however revolutionary, must demonstrate its dollars-and-cents value in the context of company circumstances and needs.

Programed Instruction:
The Basic Vocabulary

By THEODORE B. DOLMATCH

I n any new field, a technical vocabulary develops along with the
subject area itself. In programed learning, the special vocabulary
is already large, and it is still growing. Some time may be needed
before there is general agreement—even among the experts—about
the meaning of every term. It is certainly a mistake to rely on the
usual dictionary definitions, or even on any single specialist's definitions, to provide an understanding of programed instruction. The
word "programing" itself, for example, may suggest parallels between computer programing and programed instruction that do not
in fact exist. Nevertheless, a brief review of some of the key concepts and the terms most generally used to designate them will
serve to make discussion easier and more consistent.

COMMON WORDS AND PHRASES

In programed instruction, a *program* is a sequence of *items, steps,*
or *frames* which presents material to the learner. Each frame contains new information and/or a recapitulation of information, com-
bined with some material requiring a response (called the *stimulus*).
This may be a question, a fill-in, or a problem to be solved. The size
of each frame varies with the programing technique used and with
the special requirements of the subject matter.

After each of his responses, the learner is provided with information about the correctness, quality, or appropriateness of his re-

13

sponse (*feedback*). On the basis of this feedback, the learner determines whether or not he has grasped the material. Since the material in each frame is carefully structured and builds very precisely on preceding information, errors should be minimal. Thus the learner has the *reward* of being frequently correct. This gratification is both *reinforcement* and a stimulus to future learning.

Since the learner is continuously involved and is guided toward learning by the nature of the material itself (aided sometimes by *augmenting statements* or by *prompts*), programed instruction is said to *control behavior* during the learning process.

Basic to every program, according to the *NEA Journal*, are controlled presentation of material, the active response of the learner, the use of *cues* (prompts) to elicit the correct responses, immediate confirmation of success or failure, and reinforcement of correct responses to encourage the individual learner to move ahead at his own pace from familiar material to some previously determined terminal point.

The Major Approaches

Just as it is easy to become confounded by the jargon, so we can too easily become partisans of one or another of the various schools of programing to the exclusion of the others. This partisanship can result in our stressing the differences among the various techniques, rather than in our using any and all methodologies that help us reach our goal: learning.

One of the major approaches to programing follows principles enunciated by Dr. B. F. Skinner, a professor of psychology at Harvard. It is distinguished by its use of two techniques, both designed to produce rapid, error-free learning:

1. A *linear* or single-track form. The program is designed to lead the student through the material in an unbroken sequence of steps. This is differentiated from the *branching* form of programing, which provides parallel tracks onto which the student moves if he chooses an answer other than that which is considered the "best" one.
2. The *constructed response*. The student is required to compose his own response to each question (or other testing opportu-

nity). A fill-in would be a typical constructed response. This type of response should be differentiated from that which requires the learner to choose one from a number of possible— that is, rational but not necessarily true—responses already provided in the text (*multiple-choice*).

Skinnerian programers believe that errors inhibit or are *aversive* to learning. By making each step in the learning process small, by using prompts, and by basing each small increment of learning on previously learned material, they reduce the chance that the student will fail to grasp the information correctly. Therefore, they also reduce the chance that the student's constructed response will be incorrect. While these programs need not be completely error-free, the number of possible errors should be rigorously controlled.

Another approach to programing, that favored by Norman A. Crowder, employs the multiple-choice response and generally provides more information per frame. Learners who make the wrong choice from among those presented find themselves shunted onto another track or branch which corrects their error or further clarifies the point in question. The branching sequence may continue for a number of frames, again depending on the student's responses, before the learner finds himself back on the main track. Crowder's *intrinsic programing* focuses on determining whether the communication of information from program to learner is successful, and through branching provides a remedy in case of failure.

As programing techniques develop and other specialists enter this growing field, certain combinations of techniques are appearing that make classification more and more difficult. Thus there are now linear programs which contain multiple-choice frames, and there are basically linear programs with branching sequences. This development reinforces the belief that the major differences between Skinner and Crowder lie more in the realm of philosophy than in the kind of track or in the kind of stimulus provided.

NOTE: This seems as fitting a point as any to mention the controversy between "programed" and "programmed" instruction. With manufacturers, practitioners, and writers entrenched on either side, the unfortunate editor stands no chance of pleasing everybody.

Occasionally, preference for one or the other spelling is mild. Richard J. Morse, a contributor to this volume, sounded us out a little wistfully: "I have noticed . . . that you people spell 'programming' with just one *m* whereas I use two. This is not really a critical point, but I find it interesting." Others, we are afraid, would disagree sharply with Mr. Morse's view of the problem as "not really critical"; nor, as they see it, is "interesting" the right adjective. For example, one correspondent wrote from Basic Systems, Inc., "I respectfully urge you to spell 'programmed' and 'programming' with two *m*'s rather than one."

There seems no hope of resolving the difficulty short of Presidential edict. In the early days of electronic data processing, editors encountered the same problem but managed to drift along amicably: computer program(m)ers and other EDP specialists didn't seem to mind much what we did—possibly because the controversial words didn't occur in every line as they seem to when we talk about program(m)ed instruction. So—coached, we suspect, by other editors—the authorities have lined up. Take a random selection of manufacturers and marketers alone. Besides Basic Systems, U.S. Industries, Rheem, Thompson Ramo Wooldridge, and Encyclopaedia Britannica Films insist on the double *m;* while Grolier, General Education, Industrial Education, and American Systems favor just one.

To judge from absolutely unsupported personal impression, it would appear that the proponents of two *m*'s have the weight of numbers on their side. Frequently they back up their choice by claiming that the single *m* leads to ambiguities in pronunciation. "Programer," they say, looks as though it ought to be pronounced "prograymer." And some of them may be influenced by the British "programme" for "program"—there is a sizable, though diminishing, body of opinion in this country which holds that British usage is somehow more correct and certainly more elegant than the American.

In the United States, however, the rule calls for retaining the single consonant when a verb, in its simple form, consists of two syllables and is accented on the first. Thus: "program, programed, programer, programing" (like "travel, traveled, traveler, traveling"). Most dictionaries give these spellings first, although they allow the double consonant as well. AMA's editors have therefore decided to stick with the rule and "programed" instruction. That is the spelling used throughout this book—except, of course, in the bibliography, where chaos reigns.

In making this decision, we have pleased at least one of our contributors. C. D. Leatherman writes: "I'm *glad* that you have dropped the extra *m* in 'programed instruction.'" And, as Dr. Leatherman adds, Webster also approves.

A Managerial Perspective on Programed Instruction

By THEODORE B. DOLMATCH

The typical position description for the job of "training director" very likely includes a statement that the training director's responsibilities include "keeping informed about new methods and techniques for training."

Teaching machines and programed learning have been very much in the news lately. Both the popular press and the business magazines have reported on these new instructional concepts. Meetings of training specialists have been held, till by now it is quite clear that the training director must look into teaching machines and programed learning in order to meet his responsibilities and capitalize on his opportunities.

Shortly after he gets involved in the field, however, the training man may become disenchanted. The jargon, the number of new gimmicks and gadgets, and the expense of some of the paraphernalia to his mind add up to one thing: Teaching machines and programed learning—whatever they may offer—are something he can do without for the time being. Perhaps he can be sold on them later, but not now.

There is no doubt that, like many other new areas of inquiry, programed learning has its special terminology, its cabalistic expertise, and its marginal practitioners. The field seems to be growing so quickly that self-professed experts are having a field day, everyone wants to get into the act, and some undercapitalized and undertalented entrepreneurs see only the opportunity for a quick dollar.

17

The idea that this field is something very complicated and arcane, requiring the help of costly advisers, is a very attractive idea—for those advisers. The phrase "teaching machine" itself calls to mind boxes full of electronic gadgetry, and the cost of some of these teaching machines is enough—despite projected savings—to make strong controllers weep.

Nevertheless, programed instruction is a significant new tool for the training director, and it may be helpful to try to put it in its proper perspective—proper for the training director and the executive, that is. The educational psychologist and the research man have their own special requirements, but it should be helpful to avoid some of the complexity that a consideration of their needs always seems to produce.

Wrong Choice of Words

To make a start, it might be best to avoid the phrase "teaching machine" altogether. It is an attractive combination of words, calling to mind flashing lights and robots. It seems to imply an application of modern technology to that old-fashioned process called "learning." However, it is misleading, and we might be better off if it had never been invented.

If a "teaching machine" is a man-made device that instructs, then a book is a teaching machine, and so is an educational film or recording. So are the Link trainer, the mockups of company products and equipment used in many training programs, and other simulation mechanisms, some of them very elaborate. Since "teaching machine" can describe so many different instructional devices, whether or not any new concepts or principles are involved, many producers of films, tapes, and records have set themselves up as teaching-machine specialists. And it is the rare "teaching-machine exhibit" that does not include instructional devices in rapid and remedial reading, foreign-language records, and similar helpful tools. How natural it is for some producers of these instructional devices to pick up the fashionable designation, dropping the old label until the time comes to pick it up again. How natural, too, for the user of instructional aids to be confused and irritated.

The term "teaching machine" produces an unfortunate reaction in many people. Some teachers see themselves becoming obsolete because of this new-fangled machine, and some training directors wonder secretly whether they too will be casualties of automation. Their feelings are similar to those the accountant had when he was first faced with the computer. Indeed, the same training director who once gave courses to accounting personnel designed to allay the fears of technological change may now need the same sort of re-assurance he provided for them.

He can have them. He and the teacher will not be replaced any more than the accountant was. As a matter of fact, there are few parallels between the effects of the data-processing machine and the teaching machine except those suggested by the unfortunate term "teaching machine" itself. The chief similarities are two: First, this kind of instruction may accelerate learning just as data processing speeded up data collection. Second, it should upgrade the job of the training man, just as EDP upgraded the financial and informa-tion-gathering functions. But these similarities are fortuitous, and they are not enhanced by the designation "teaching machine."

The term has one other major disadvantage. It gratuitously pro-vides ammunition for the pseudo-intellectuals who persist in seeing teaching as a mystical communion between teacher (in tweeds with pipe) and student (with shining eyes). In an era of extensive mechanization, are we to automate that last citadel of the intellect —teaching? Even if the answer is a clear "no," the purist may still react viscerally to that loaded word "machine."

The Case for "Programed Instruction"

It may be optimistic to hope that the "teaching machine" idea will lose its fascination, particularly since the Sunday supplements are addicted to such catchy concepts. In any case, a much better term is "programed instruction," for it describes what is being done and has appropriate overtones of the organized, systematic approach to the act of instruction which is the key to this new method.

Programed instruction, as the term is used here, means more than the simple ordering of course material. It is instruction that meets these specific criteria:

1. It is individualized; that is, one person learns at a time. The

device speaks to him without the intercession of a monitor or tutor.

2. The device presents material to be learned in minimal increments. It operates on the principle that we learn better in small doses, and that we also learn better if we avoid error. By proceeding in small steps, we obviously reduce the likelihood of error.

3. That which is to be taught is rigorously ordered. Because of the desire to hold errors to an absolute or pre-ordained minimum, each step in the learning process has to follow logically, as well as closely, the one preceding it.

4. Students progress at their own pace. Instead of being restricted to a classroom situation where the norm of learning must become the pace of every student in the room, each user of a programed instructional device learns as quickly as he is able. His rate of accomplishment is established by his performance alone.

5. The student's answer is almost instantaneously checked against the correct response, which appears before the next question is asked. In this way, the student receives the reassurance that his answer (response) is correct, and the very appearance of the correct answer reinforces his learning. If the answer is incorrect, he can easily locate the reason for his error, without, as in traditional learning, discovering that he is—all at once— at sea.

Any instructional device can be accepted or rejected on its own merits, whether or not it meets these five criteria. Calling any audiovisual or other educational tool a "teaching machine" does not make it one, and even if all these criteria are met, it is optimistic to assume that programed instruction, simply by virtue of its *being* programed instruction, teaches any better or any worse than other kinds of instruction.

There are good and bad programs, just as there are good and bad teachers. The good ones do the job well, and the poorest are probably worse than nothing at all. At this time, in the infancy of programed instruction, we are more likely to find programs that do not meet our standards, but this should not deter us from searching out the good programs and benefiting from them.

Keys to the Evaluation Problem

Determining which *are* the good programs is vital, and it is not much more difficult than determining the quality of any other brand of instruction. Evaluation, in short, requires pre-established standards. Most instruction has as its goal *changed behavior,* but it is rather discouraging to note how little this goal is analyzed or even considered when the quality of instruction is measured. The academic world can, if it chooses, evaluate teaching by counting its teachers' advanced degrees and frequency of publication, by having supervisors make annual classroom visits, or by similar criteria. Teaching in industry cannot be weighed by these factors.

Industry is, in fact, more fortunate than the college in this respect. We need not rely on examinations for data. We have many more valid measurements of performance, if we will identify and use them. The great amount of numerical data available to us, the graphs, charts, and balance sheets that are a fundamental part of industry, should be our starting point. Management cannot afford to accept intuition as a measure, and it has no need to do so.

The need for evaluation in the training department is of course not confined to its use of programed instruction. Every kind of training, every method, every approach is amenable to proper testing and should be evaluated in this way. It is not surprising that so much industrial training is done on faith; the analogue we find in the academic world encourages us to accept it without question. But faith isn't enough. In industry, we train in order to produce more and better products, and we have production and quality control records to tell us whether we are getting them. We train to get more work done per hour, and time records tell us whether we are succeeding. We train to get better supervisors, and in addition to these production, quality control, and time data we have attendance, grievance, turnover, maintenance, safety, and many other records with which to measure our supervision. Finally, we have balance sheets and a variety of financial records—the payoff—which provide a kind of final examination for the company as a whole.

Improvement in performance, demonstrated by positive changes in these data, is the goal of training. It is the training director's job to search out the correlations between his program and performance

—not to manufacture the correlations or ride along on the coattails of a recession that reduces turnover, absenteeism, or grievances. And it is also his job to provide the best possible training to produce improved performance.

THE CONFLICT OF THE THEORISTS

In his search for effective training methods, the specialist has discovered programed instruction. Experiments in schools and in the military indicate that it is truly an important new concept, with applications of great potential significance to business and industrial training. It is also a new concept with a great many conflicting theories and practices. Should the program be "linear," "branching," multiple-choice, or what have you? What subject matter is appropriate for programing? Who will help us construct a program?

At this time, one of the most unrewarding of practices is for the average training man to attempt to become an expert in programing itself. A few pioneer training departments are in fact developing programers within the company, and the day may come when industry will handle its own program construction as a matter of course, but that day isn't here yet. Some directors may be interested in finding out all about the conflicting schools of programing and the complex experimentation that has influenced their thinking and is still going on; for them, the bibliography at the end of this book will give an idea of the available literature.* I have a feeling, however, that too much concern with theory might complicate the complicated and allow the primary job—getting improved performance—to be sidetracked, perhaps forever.

As a matter of fact, the odds are great that much of the current conflict among the theorists will be resolved as more programs are issued and evaluated. At present, many of the companies working in the field seem more interested in the "machines" than in the instruction.

* I would recommend three books in particular: (1) Lumsdaine, A.A., and Robert Glaser (editors), *Teaching Machines and Programmed Learning: A Source Book*, National Education Association, Department of Audio-Visual Instruction, Washington, D. C., 1960; (2) Lysaught, Jerome P. (editor), *Programmed Learning: Evolving Principles and Industrial Applications*, The Foundation for Research on Human Behavior, Ann Arbor, Michigan, 1961; (3) Galanter, Eugene (editor), *Automatic Teaching: The State of the Art*, John Wiley & Sons, New York, 1959.

A More Logical Emphasis

There may be a parallel here in the development of the safety razor. When it first appeared, it was an expensive device; the blades were very much an afterthought. It eventually became clear, however, that not only did the blade do the shaving but there was more money in blades. And there was also something to be said for blades which fitted many different razors.

In terms of marketing, it would seem logical for the companies involved in programed learning to emphasize the program rather than the device carrying it—the blade, rather than the razor. This doesn't seem to be the case now, although some purveyors of programed learning (shall we call them "manufacturers," "publishers," "programers," or what?) are beginning to pay more attention to the material itself. The time may come, of course, when the program—complete and ready for use—will be available as a unit that includes its own "machinery."

Such a unit has already been achieved by certain book publishers, who have issued "scrambled books" or programs that look like books on the outside but have text pages designed according to the principles of programed learning. Unfortunately, these programed books are somewhat unwieldy to use, and they do not motivate the learner as some of the machines do. Indeed, even though one would wish otherwise, the "look of the book" seems to have negative effects on many students, regardless of the look of the inside pages.

Experimentation now going on indicates the probability of new devices that will be less expensive than some that are now being sold. It also seems most likely that the form of the particular device may eventually depend on the program it carries. Thus programing an assembly operation may require a machine that includes motion pictures, special earphones, and other complex attachments—and be very much worthwhile—while programing a course in supervision may call for no more than a text which a man can carry in his pocket.

Constructors of programs, now arguing over the relative merits of branching or linear methods, may find that some subjects require one technique, some another. Or they may discover that both methods can combine to provide better instruction than either alone. Or, as they learn more about the subject, they may find that a new method, neither linear nor branching, works better yet. The test lies in the student's responses, not in the theoretician's.

In short, the validation, not the organization, of the program is the key to its use.

What Can a Company Do?

At the present time, with so many variations among programs and machines, it seems questionable whether a company should commit itself to large capital expenditures for instructional apparatus. There are, of course, certain specific situations where a particular machine program, whose efficacy in similar circumstances has already been demonstrated, may be called for. Much experimentation with programed learning can be done by paper-and-pencil methods, however.

If the manual devices somehow do not reproduce the motivation of the electronic gadgets, that is too bad—but it also may be more realistic to face facts from the start. Every new gadget supplies, while it is new, a special motivation: people like to play with it. This motivation may speed learning now, but it is likely to wear off as the gadget becomes familiar. Even the paper devices provide some incentives based on their newness and format, but why evaluate the success of an instructional device on the basis of evanescent advantages?

It also seems likely that experimentation will reveal that certain subjects can be best taught by one kind of program, that other subjects call for another kind, and that still other subjects call for combinations of programing methods that now seem to be incompatible.

It would seem appropriate for the training specialist to try different kinds of programs—for skill training, for supervisory development, and for all the other training areas for which he is responsible. He should, for economies in time and money, select those that seem immediately applicable and are the work of well-known producers of sound programed materials. He should search for validation, but he should try not to be too impressed by studies which prove that carefully structured programed instruction produces better results than "traditional" instruction. The real question is *what kind* of traditional methods were used. Ideally, we should compare different methods of similar quality, but how often has this been done so far?

ARGUMENTS IN FAVOR OF PROGRAMING

Even if a good program and good traditional instruction produce the same level of performance and the same retention of knowledge, there may be very good reasons to use programed instruction in industry whenever possible.

First, the time spent in conventional training costs a great deal of money. It is time taken away from production time. If programed instruction speeds learning, then it is a cost-cutting (time-saving) tool of great significance.

Second, the consistency of the program—with each learner getting the same material—may solve many problems. The swing shift can expect to be taught as well as the day shift, even though the best human instructor is home with his family. Equivalent training should produce equivalent performance, which is always desirable.

Third, since programed instruction is a solo affair, the juggling of schedules to get a class together is unnecessary. And each learner gets his training at his own pace, so that the fast students can be made productive more rapidly, without being held back by the class.

Fourth, programed instruction by its design provides a great deal of motivation beyond that supplied by the device itself. It sets up a situation in which the student is virtually compelled to learn by the subtle pressures of the program and his desire to learn is increased by immediate reinforcement.

Finally, programed instruction gives the training director a new role in industry. He can subordinate his role as instructor, attendance-checker, and test administrator. Relieved of these tasks, he can spend more time searching for the correlations between training and performance, refining his courses of instruction to increase their tie-in with actual company needs. He can identify the specific areas needing more instruction and help the students in the precise areas where they are having special difficulty. In short, like the finance man with EDP, he has a new tool to help him and a new competency through which he can help his company.

Programed Instruction in the Framework of Company Training

By ELIZABETH MARTING

I f a company president had dropped out of sight in 1947 only to be reunited with his grateful subordinates 15 years later, he would be amazed at what he saw.

He might, in fact, find his organization almost obliterated by successive mergers. Even if it were more or less recognizable, he might still be bewildered at the products it was turning out. In the plant, he would marvel at changes in process and production methods; beginning with the single word "automation," he would have to learn a whole new vocabulary. In the office, he would be faced with electronic equipment of terrifying complexity and a concept of management in which the gathering and sorting of data played a major role. He would be astonished to hear his people speak casually of marketing and even manufacturing operations from Afghanistan to the Zambesi—though not so casually of the danger to U.S. industry of foreign competition not only overseas but, of all places, at home. And he would be dumbfounded at the extent to which he appeared to be involved in education, in something called "development."

As president, our man would no doubt become aware of this last phenomenon first of all among his executive group. He might, for example, go down the hall to see the controller in his office and be told by a secretary that the controller was off attending a week's seminar in interpersonal relations. "But how can we get along without him? Who's doing his work?" the president would almost certainly ask. "Oh, we're getting along," the secretary might reply. "Besides, sir, this seminar is so important that the company thought it would be worth the lost time."

"The *company?*" might conceivably be the president's reaction before he discovered that management had made surprising progress in the direction of professionalization during his absence; that his top-level executives not only worried about "developing" their subordinates but exposed themselves periodically to courses, seminars, and conferences in various aspects of management. What's more, the company not only condoned the time away from the job but paid all the expenses. Then, as he looked more closely, our president might find that a great deal of "development" was taking place within the company, particularly among first-line supervisors. It might strike him too, when he got to the rank and file, that the amount of company time, money, and energy expended in the name of manpower development and training was incredible—and that some of the subject matter had very little to do with the job. At which point, seeking out the executive vice president who had carried on loyally during all those 15 years, he might well ask, "Why?"

Growing Sophistication

It is a fact that the manpower-development effort in industry *has* proliferated over the past decade and a half. Further, it is becoming more sophisticated. This is as true in the small and medium-sized company as it is in the large firm where a full-time training staff has sprung up; the training resources available to business and industry are so varied that the smaller organization has had no difficulty in adapting them to its needs and purse. But why all this interest and effort? As our executive vice president might have said simply, "It's the thing to do! Everybody's gotten into it—we couldn't afford to stay out!" On a more serious level, he could have given his chief several reasons why training had assumed such importance for the company and—provided the program was sound—added firmly that it was paying off.

What are these reasons? There are four that might be cited,

although they are so completely intertwined and interrelated that each is both cause and effect.

1. *The inadequacies of our present-day educational system.* The charges brought against the American school system need no repeating here: we have heard too often of the secretary who cannot spell and of workers who lack even the most fundamental understanding of our economic system. But the problem of insufficient preparation extends, also, to engineers and other highly educated technical personnel who cannot make an effective oral or written report and to liberal arts graduates whose background is beyond reproach but who need specific skills to get ahead in business.

2. *The scarcity of trained manpower of all types and at all levels.* This is a problem that forecasters and statisticians warn us will grow worse before it improves. Whatever factors are responsible—the low birth rate of the 1930's, the impact of war, the increasing proportion of retired workers—it means that companies will have to hire more and more inexperienced workers and hope that, with training, they can be transformed into real producers. Presently, and for the foreseeable future, the great need is for management talent.

3. *The growing complexity of many jobs.* As is frequently pointed out, the technological revolution which is now in progress is upgrading some jobs just as it is abolishing others. There is going to be less and less opportunity for unskilled labor. To answer to society for the displacement of whole classes of workers by machines, and to help employees meet the new demands being made on them, companies will have to expand their training programs.

4. *The mutually profitable exchange of personnel and ideas between the educational and industrial training worlds.* Many company trainers have had their start in the schools and universities. Many line employees have served time as trainers, liked the work, and stayed on—fascinated by the ferment of new concepts, subject areas, and techniques. Educators are gregarious, whether in industry or in academia, with the result that, as the typical training effort has grown, it has also increased its over-all effectiveness.

Receptiveness to Innovation

One factor in this increased effectiveness has undoubtedly been the readiness of training specialists—particularly those in companies which have become leaders in the training field—to experiment with new teaching methods and devices. There have been fads, true, in both subject matter and tools, but staff training people have improved their own skills steadily and have succeeded remarkably well in sharing a part of their knowledge with the line managers and supervisors who are basically responsible for training in any company. In particular, they have made available an imposing array of supplementary teaching aids and accustomed personnel at all levels to their use.

Educators have long realized the value of appealing to the student's eyes as well as his ears and mind. Hence the use in industrial training of such visual aids as the blackboard, color slides, motion pictures, models or actual samples of company products and equipment. Some of these aids have been refined and elaborated on; for instance, the need for greater flexibility in presenting charts, diagrams, and key words has led from the traditional blackboard and padboard to such variations as flannelboard, corkboard, pegboard, magnetic board, even "hook and eye" board. Joseph Arthur, director of industrial education for The Timken Roller Bearing Company, says that hardly a session in supervisory or management development is held in his organization without the help of a flannelboard—indeed, it is a brave lecturer or conference leader in any company who would face a group without one.

Industrial training of course has many facets, dealing as it must with people of varying backgrounds, abilities, and levels of education. At the one extreme is management development, about which, perhaps, most has been heard in recent years. It is typical of company training and personnel people, and of their backers in top management, that they were quick to see how management education, as it developed after World War II, filled a serious and a growing need. Typically, too, they have seized upon tools and techniques which showed promise. Take, as a single example, decision simulation: the so-called management "game." In spite of the large number in industry and in business schools today, and in spite of widespread attempts at evaluation, the consensus at present seems to be that the device has not yet proved itself, although certainly it is capable on occasion of whipping participants into an extraordinary state of excitement. But what would our returned company president say if he walked in on a dozen highly paid executives spending expensive hours over a "game"?

And in any case management development, while it may lately have seemed like the frosting on the cake, is *only* the frosting. It represents a relatively small part of the total company training effort; there remain the problems of enabling and encouraging technical personnel to keep up to date in their specialties, of training new employees and retraining old ones to assume new and more challenging assignments, of developing supervisors to function more fully through the whole range of their assigned duties and, especially, to accept their responsibility for on-the-job coaching and training. The company may, if it chooses, delegate part of this tremendous training load by calling in outside specialists or making judicious arrangements with nearby educational institutions. In some areas of training, either may provide a satisfactory solution, particularly for the small company whose personnel and funds are limited. But the more closely the subject matter of training is related to job content, the more personally company people—above all, supervisors—must concern themselves with it.

NEEDED: GREATER IMPACT AND PERMANENCY

Jerome B. Lysaught, speaking at a recent AMA conference of Eastman Kodak's experience as a pioneer in this field, said that

> . . . a few people are resistant to programed learning in any shape or form. There are, as a matter of fact, two general categories of people who are unhappy. One group is unhappy because, generally speaking, its members have habitually been very successful students and have attributed their success to standard textbooks and standard human instructors; they feel that programed learning is a sad substitute for these two accepted ways of exchanging information.

> A second group of people who are not happy with programed learning consists essentially of those who are upset by the use of the teaching

machine. These people may be willing to use programed textbooks and workbooks, but they feel somehow they have been precipitated into the year 1984 when they sit down in front of a machine. . . .

If this is so, can't the reverse be true as well? In other words, if outstandingly successful students and people who distrust machines don't like programed instruction, aren't we justified in supposing that people who are not outstanding students and who *like* machines will be favorably disposed toward it?

These people, after all, are in the majority not only in the average company but in the world at large. This means that the typical supervisor-trainer will in all probability be dealing for the most part with people who are not receptive to "learning," who resisted it all through their school careers and are not much minded to welcome it now. The supervisor himself may very well be similarly minded; in any event, those responsible for training in the company will surely have as raw material a preponderance of trainees in this category.

That is why training directors constantly seek new means of presenting material more vividly, of making a greater impact, of achieving more permanent results. That is why, in addition to making the use of *visual* aids a fine science, they have added an *audio* element by introducing sound films, seizing on the tape recorder, even experimenting—in spite of the expense—with closed-circuit TV. That is why they are now looking with eager interest, and in growing numbers, at a programed instruction and teaching machines.

The Field Surveyed: First Steps Toward Programed Industrial Training

By ELIZABETH MARTING

Which are the companies that have taken the lead in exploring the possibilities of programed instruction and teaching machines? Their first, in most cases rather tentative, applications have been reported with considerable excitement both in the business magazines and in the scholarly publications followed by those concerned with the behavioral sciences. They tend, obviously, to be companies that have chronic training problems.

These problems may be product-related. Take the manufacturers of jet aircraft and allied equipment, of radar and other devices essential to the country's defense, of cameras and optical goods, of highly complex electronic data-processing machines. From the development standpoint alone, they make phenomenal demands on human knowledge and ingenuity. The shortage of scientists and engineers being what it is, companies must resign themselves to making do with available talent and seeing that any deficiencies in background are eliminated as fast as possible by in-company or company-sponsored training. There is, in any event, the need to orient all newly hired technical personnel to the company's special requirements; no engineering school, for example, can be expected to turn out graduates who will be thoroughly at home in whatever specialized field. Moreover, technical people at all stages of their careers must be encouraged and helped to keep up to date. The narrower their specialty as time goes on, the more important it becomes that they keep abreast of new thinking and practice outside the immediate job environment.

32

Product complexity poses training problems, also, for production management. Workers in most cases have only a modest amount of schooling and, too often, no real understanding of the job they are doing as it relates to the over-all operation and no sense of responsibility for results. Turnover is high, particularly among girls and women, and a prolonged period of training is just not feasible. Yet equipment may be delicate, expensive, and easily damaged; precision and other specifications must be met; schedules are generally tight; and the cost of rejects, in time and money, is frequently excessive.

Allied to the manufacturer's production-line problem is that of many service industries which necessarily employ great numbers of clerical or operating personnel. In this group are insurance companies, public utilities, banks, department stores, mail order houses. A relatively large proportion of the workforce in the typical organization consists of girls and women. Again, job tenure tends to be short; telephone companies, for instance, must recruit continuously, in spite of increasing automation, to keep their lines staffed. Again, qualifications cannot be set too high, and extended training is out of the question. At the same time, however, the work must be done quickly and accurately. Frequently, as in banks, it involves figures, and while office mechanization may have lessened the burden of detail in some respects, the machines' very complexity has created new problems and accentuated old ones. And in service industries the element of customer satisfaction is supremely important: the bank balance must be correct, the insurance premium credited to the right policyholder, the transatlantic toll call properly billed, the correct merchandise supplied in the asked-for style, color, size, and quantity.

Mention of the customer brings us to the salesman, who in many industries must be more than an amiable order-taker. He must know his product so thoroughly as to be able to determine its potential value to a specific customer, sell that potential to the customer within the limits of propriety and business integrity, and stand by through the adjustment period to see that the product, once delivered, lives up to expectations. Where it is designed to order, he becomes a sales engineer and must be equipped accordingly; the manufacturers of electronic data-processing systems have been

particularly concerned to develop trained sales and service representatives. In addition, a *new* product calls for special marketing
effort. Among others, the country's pharmaceutical houses—faced
with intensified competition in "miracle" and "wonder" drugs—are
coaching their sales staffs more and more carefully in the presentation of their products to doctors, hospitals, and druggists.

Heightened competition in all areas of business and industry has,
in fact, aggravated these varied training problems almost universally.
They are problems which, in spite of small differences from company
to company, are basically similar. It is no accident that in lists of
programed subjects and courses such titles as "Algebra," "Basic
Electronics," and "Computer Programing" recur over and over. For
programed instruction, it has seemed to many personnel and training specialists, offers the promise of better—and more permanent—
results than have heretofore been achieved.

Two Pioneers

Two companies' initial applications of programed instruction have
had such widespread publicity as to minimize any need for dis-
cussing them in detail here. These companies are IBM and Eastman
Kodak. In both, seemingly, the results have been measurable in
terms of class time, learning achievement, and employee acceptance
and have encouraged the extension of programed instruction into
further courses and subject areas—always with critical evaluation
as compared to traditional methods of teaching.

Eastman Kodak Company.[1] In Eastman Kodak we have one of the
many companies whose training people were first alerted to new
concepts of learning by becoming acquainted with the studies of
Dr. B. F. Skinner of the Harvard Psychological Laboratories.

The company began tentatively to program selected training materials some four years ago. It soon became evident, says Jerome P.
Lysaught, that "material organized and presented by means of programed instruction lived up to the theoretical possibilities indicated
by evidence collected in Dr. Skinner's laboratories. That is, we

---

[1] For a full discussion of Eastman Kodak's experience with programed instruction
see Margulies, S., and Lewis Eigen (editors), *Programed Instruction*, John Wiley
& Sons, Inc., New York, 1962.

found that people were motivated to learn; that immediate knowledge of results promoted learning; and that by working at their own individual rate, through a carefully sequenced series of items, people could achieve understanding of the subject matter."

Since then the programing activity has increased to the point where the Eastman Kodak Company now has four full-time programers and a dozen other employees who, working part-time, have prepared programed materials. Furthermore, the company has a subsidiary—the Recordak Corporation—which is considering the possibility of the manufacture and marketing of teaching machines which, unsurprisingly, would use microfilm to store and present their subject matter.

About 20 programed sequences have been developed for various areas of training at Kodak, ranging from supervisory management to the technical aspects of photography. This broad range was encouraged deliberately to learn whether there might be areas of industrial training to which programed instruction was not suited. The company reports, however, that it has yet to find and define such areas. In addition, projects to date have proved that the company can do programing and can train its own programers. In fact, company personnel have been able to help the University of Rochester in training 150 classroom teachers in programing techniques.

The Eastman Kodak approach has been, not to program whole courses initially, but to pick out certain parts of courses with which students seemed to have trouble. These have been programed first. It is possible that eventually the programed sections can be linked so as to provide complete courses—say, in basic photography. Meanwhile, Eastman Kodak is benefiting from each programed sequence as it is developed.

Students have found the programed material a challenge. They have discovered that they must take a more active part in the learning process than that to which they have been accustomed in the past. This greater effort is, of course, reflected in an increasingly high level of learning and, for some, in a more rapid mastery of the subject matter. Only a relatively few students resist programed instruction.

Many supervisors have moved from a position of skepticism to one of acceptance. For instance, in wage and salary administration, girls who were working with statistics asked their supervisors for training in the latest statistical techniques. The prescription? A six-week programed course in descriptive statistics published by TMI-Grolier. The pre-test showed percentage scores in the 40's and 50's; six weeks later the lowest score on a similar test was 93. As a result, interestingly, the department supervisors also studied the programed material.

In some cases the attitude of the company's professional trainers was at first negative. In 20 or 25 years a training man sees many fads come and go; he is understandably in no mood to welcome the newest development, accompanied by the usual drum beating, as the answer to all his problems. Now most training men are beginning to feel that programed instruction—based as it is on laboratory experience in learning behavior—will have more to offer than the gimmicks which so often have failed him in the past.

International Business Machines Corporation.[2] IBM is outstanding among those manufacturers for which product complexity and the continual development of new products have meant a steady increase in training activity. Its early experiments with programed instruction—which, as in the case of Eastman Kodak, were inspired by the work of Dr. B. F. Skinner—are fully described on pages 63-72. Here is an organization, seemingly, that intends to push ahead, to broaden its studies and see whether further applications of this new technique may not be possible—and profitable. And its efforts, again like Eastman Kodak's, are encouraging still other companies in a variety of industries to explore this new field.

Briefly Cited

If it is true, as *Business Week* reports in its issue of August 26, 1961, that "there has been no rush to programed learning," that "most of the 50 or more organizations now in the programed-learning business are aiming at the schools," and that "most companies are still just looking," it can at least be said that many companies are looking hard at the possibilities of the new tool *in relation to their own objectives and needs.*

Some are concluding—and will conclude—that programed learn-

[2] See note 1, page 34.

ing is not for them; for example, a training man in an oil-company subsidiary writes:

A programed book on statistics was tried by one of our divisions. The individuals doing the evaluating felt that the book did not tie the use of statistics to our application and in general was inferior to standard teaching techniques.

Other companies are choosing an area of training which has given trouble in the past, with traditional methods of teaching, and are experimenting to see what programed instruction can accomplish and how its effectiveness compares with that of their old methods. Some of these companies are briefly mentioned in the following paragraphs; in later sections of this book a few of them analyze their experiences for the benefit of those interested—with honest attention to the problems and disadvantages of programed instruction as well as its advantages.

Background Courses. Since, as *Business Week* says, professional programers and marketers of programed texts and teaching machines are directing most of their attention to the academic world, it comes as no surprise that many subject areas in which industrial specialists have tried programed instruction are those with which company personnel—often engineers and technical people—must be acquainted in order to improve their performance and to qualify for promotion. In some cases, these subject areas have been chosen because programed materials were commercially available or existing course outlines could readily be adapted.

Thus the Kearfott Division of General Precision, Inc., in Little Falls, New Jersey, has machine-taught algebra, trigonometry, basic electronics, and the use of the slide rule to repair-shop supervisors (pages 83-90). ACF is teaching algebra to machine apprentices by means of programed texts (pages 101-102); the Sandia Corporation is using similarly scrambled texts or looseleaf notebooks for instruction in algebra, statistics, basic electricity, and Russian (pages 73-82); while the Bell Telephone Laboratories has reportedly been experimenting with programed texts as a means of presenting introductory electricity to maintenance people in the Bell System's independent operating companies.

For all these subjects, it will be noted, companies could refer employees to convenient schools and universities. Some firms, however, because of their geographical location, the size or urgency of the training need, or a desire to relate course content more closely to job requirements, undertake to provide instruction on the premises.

Job Training and/or Guidance for Production and Product-Service Employees. What might be termed "background" merges imperceptibly into knowledge and skills which are basic to job performance. In this latter class, perhaps, are DuPont's reported use of a machine format to train personnel in blueprint reading; the System Development Corporation's teaching of computer number systems by scrambled text prior to instruction in computer programing (pages 119-123); General Telephone of California's experiment in programed training for installer-repairmen (pages 43-48); and RCA's machine-teaching of the basics of computer technology. RCA, in fact, is said to be planning its own teaching machine; if it does enter the field, it will by no means be the only company that has become interested in a product first as consumer, then as manufacturer.

The Ampex Corporation, recording-equipment maker in Redwood City, California, has used the principles of programed instruction, plus an audio-visual element, on the actual production floor. In ten work stations built by Ampex of equipment supplied by Litton Industries' Applied Communication Systems Division, girls are guided as they assemble electronic chassis for video-tape recorders.

Training for Clerical, Operating, and Customer-Service Personnel. We have already seen something of the difficulties facing insurance companies, public utilities, banks, mail order houses, department stores, and other big employers of workers who must handle a great amount of detail and who have a direct impact on customer relations. Programed instruction is being tried by numerous companies in these categories as a partial answer to the training problem.

General Telephone of California, for example, has used tape recordings to train information operators (pages 111-118); and AT&T reportedly has been programing an "auto-instructional" course in booklet form for trial use with outward toll operators in a number of offices. Spiegel, Inc., the Chicago mail order firm, is quoted as having tried a programed billing course as one of several applications —and dropped it. The reasoning seems to have been that, since the

students progressed at their own rate of speed, all were not ready
for on-the-job training at once; hence added supervisory costs over-
balanced the saving in class time. Most companies, however, like
the flexibility of individualized training and consider this one of
programed instruction's chief benefits.

In the banking industry a number of organizations have had good
results with the Reinforced Learning System developed by the
William Barton Marsh Company. A mail survey of 20 major U.S.
banks indicates that, after a minimum of three months' experience
in training IBM Model 801/803 proof machine operators by the
new method, almost all find training time is reduced, trainees attain
production speed faster, supervisors can concentrate on other responsibilities, and both supervisors and trainees appear to like the
system.

Sales Training. Traditionally, sales supervision has been notably
open-minded toward new devices for coaching salesmen in selling
techniques and acquainting them with the full range of company,
and competitive, products. Individualized indoctrination by means
of programed instruction would seem to offer a promising alterna-
tive or supplement to the periodic mass conference which has been
the rule in this field.

Among pharmaceutical firms, Schering has explored the possibilities of programed texts in preparing salesmen to explain new products to physicians, hospitals, and druggists (pages 102-105). So has
Mead Johnson (pages 105-106). In other industries, Lever Brothers
(pages 49-59) and Zenith (pages 106-107) have taken the lead.
Varian Associates has put together a 25-page scrambled booklet on
its Ortho-Mode Mixer (a device for combining electro-magnetic
waves of two different frequencies to obtain a third) for salesmen
and customers; and American-Standard's Plumbing and Heating
Division is using the Mark II AutoTutor to teach salesmen how to
sell hydronic heating (pages 91-100).

In the insurance business, programed instruction has obvious potential. More than one large company is believed to be investigating
its use. Prudential, at last word, was planning a course in the fundamentals of life insurance for new agents. For easy comparison, three
groups were to be set up: one using programed texts; a second, conventional texts; a third, teaching machines.

THE PRESENT MOOD

Probably the attitude of business and industry in general amounts
to the "more than mild optimism" which Dr. Lysaught ascribes to his
colleagues at Eastman Kodak and its subsidiary Recordak. As he told
his AMA audience:

> We feel very strongly that programed instruction shows great promise
> for industrial training. We do not feel that it is a panacea, and we do
> not feel in all cases that it is a one-for-one substitute for what we are
> doing at the present time. We feel that programing will be most im-
> portant in the years ahead if only because its very technology means
> closer examination of our goals in training and our methods of reach-
> ing those goals.
>
> . . . Each experience we have had has reinforced us in our opinion that
> there is something good in which we are making real progress, but we
> also recognize that programing initially requires great expenditures in
> faith, time, and hard work. . . .

Perhaps, as Mead Johnson suggests in a discussion of teaching
aids, the key word is "effective." If a proposed new device will bring
about greater effectiveness, use it. If not, reject it. James S. Bruce,
director of training for Eastman Kodak, put it very well when he told
AMA that

> Teaching is an old profession, and over a number of years some very
> effective techniques and methods have evolved. As in most other
> phases of our civilization, the teacher is faced with an acceleration of
> change, but new things are part of an on-going evolution of the teach-
> ing pattern and not a replacement for everything that is old. If you
> have material which can be effectively presented to your students by
> the lecture method, by movies, by laboratory exercises, by case discus-
> sions, by all means use these techniques. To say that programed learn-
> ing is going to replace them all is, I think, fatuous nonsense. On the
> other hand, there are certain areas where programed learning may be
> by far the most effective method of getting information and knowledge
> across. Here, obviously, it should be used.

COMPANY THINKING ... AND ADVICE

Closer acquaintance with programed instruction appears to induce a tempered enthusiasm in most industrial trainers plus a strong urge to communicate their experience, their hopes and reservations, to colleagues in other companies.

Programed Training as We See It

By RICHARD J. MORSE

A company which does not thoroughly understand its current training problems and needs must first accomplish this awesome task before even beginning to think in terms of programed learning or training. It is ridiculous to take existing material for training in any subject and begin programing it before we first do several things. Let us see what those things are.

PRESENT TRAINING COST AND EFFECTIVENESS

In order to be able to project the amount of saving to be achieved through programing existing instructional material, we must first have an accurate figure of the current cost on which to base our comparison. Training cost is sizable and, I believe, far greater than most executives realize. Too often trainers are under extreme and constant pressure to create a particular end product—a trained employee—as quickly as possible; they cannot concern themselves with expense and effectiveness as much as they should. Soon training becomes routine, and nobody ever bothers to evaluate and analyze its effectiveness; the rut is established. We must, I repeat, know how much training costs now and how effective it is.

RICHARD J. MORSE is Instructional Methods Administrator for the General Telephone Company of California, in Santa Monica.

Effectiveness is best measured in terms of the employee's subsequent success on the job if, in fact, the training program is specifically oriented to the particular job we are training the employee for —which, of course, it should be. It is not always easy to relate job performance to learning received through training, but it is something which can and must be done before programing is considered.

Does the Current Program Accomplish Its Objectives?

It is very easy to skim through ten books on electricity, pick one which looks "pretty good," and use it in a training program designed to teach employees the basic elements of electricity, but in following this approach are we not really designing our course around the book instead of designing our training materials around the specific aspects of electricity which *we* want to teach? It is of critical importance that we determine what behavior we want the trainee to be displaying after he completes the training. In other words, we must be certain that the training material is really accomplishing the objectives it is supposed to accomplish. The only way this will happen is if the objectives are first written out and the course content is truly an expansion of these objectives.

If we do determine (as we probably will) that the existing training program does not completely do the job for which it is intended, then obviously we do not want to consider programing its content as it currently exists. It is amazing how far off track many training programs are found to be when a careful analysis is made of what the real terminal behavior—that is, the objectives—ought to be.

Is the Content Suited to the Trainees?

The more use we get from a stable training program, the more important it becomes, so that what and how we teach are critical to more of the student population. If, however, the content of the course is constantly changing and thus requires frequent revision, then our task as instructors or content writers or programers becomes more complicated.

One of the greatest advantages of programing occurs when the student population is large and is constantly changing in its make-up. However, one of the greatest disadvantages occurs when the course content is constantly changing. There is a happy medium, but it varies with each training situation, and the facts must be known for each situation so that it may be evaluated properly.

What Is the Best Method for Teaching the Material?

Before we automatically conclude that programing our training material is *the* key, we must be certain that we have not overlooked another, more effective technique or combination of techniques. At least we may discover that a combination of several teaching techniques will do the job best. Once again it is important to know our objectives.

These questions we have posed are the most important ones to be answered thoroughly before thinking about programing. There are many more, but to answer these few is a monumental task in itself. Who said it was not difficult to decide whether training subjects should be programed or not? Most of the battle is in the preliminary planning and deciding on objectives.

Training Program for Installer-Repairmen

Realizing that the tremendous cost of training is a reality, we at General Telephone Company of California decided in November 1960 to explore the utilization of programed instruction in our training classes. After researching the subject quite thoroughly and talking with many professionals in the field, we conducted a pilot study to determine the effectiveness of in-company programed-instruction training. From among our 800 installer-repairmen (the employees who install and repair our subscribers' instruments) we selected three groups of 14 members each. The members of these groups were equal in experience in the company, in prior knowledge about the subject to be taught, and in intelligence. The course material was a commercially available program. One group learned the material in book form, the second group used a teaching machine, and the third was taught the material in the same sequence as that of the programed course but in a classroom and through lectures, the method normally used by a company instructor.

The results of this initial study were not only interesting but revealing. Both program-trained groups learned as well as (but not better than) the lecture-trained group. On a retention examination given six weeks after completion of the training, the two program-trained groups retained as much as (but not more than) the lecture-trained group. The two program-trained groups took about 45 per cent less *learning* time to cover the material but only about 30 per cent less total time, because it was necessary to schedule their lessons in a different time sequence.

Although no instructor as such was needed or used for the program-trained groups, a monitor who was familiar with the course content was present in each. This proved necessary, for on several occasions the students required help in order to proceed. The majority of the students in the program-trained groups thoroughly enjoyed the experience, and they were motivated to take more such courses.

Although we were most pleased with the results, we realized that we would have to program most of our material internally rather than rely on commercially available programs. This is true because of the unique nature of many of our training requirements as well as the specific content which must be learned. The results impressed our farsighted management so much that we have its permission not only to make further experiments but also to implement our training with programed materials.

FUTURE TRAINING PLANS

We are currently examining 13 specific areas of training within our company. In cooperation with a local university we intend to train employees in programing the training material for these 13 areas. We are, in other words, selecting the actual doers of the work —the supervisors and the trainers themselves. After being trained in the skills of programing, they will write sequences, working alone and in teams. Their progress will be thoroughly evaluated.

We are studying the opinions of more than 200 experts to try to determine the selection criteria for successful programers. The composite of these characteristics, coupled with the findings of our own efforts, we hope will give us some guidelines for predicting who will be successful programers. Through these efforts we should not only evolve several good programs in various subjects but also produce several trained and capable programers. I can see only the brightest future for programed learning—not just in our company but throughout industry. We are on the brink of what I feel will be a substantial revolution in our training practices.

USEFUL BY-PRODUCTS OF PROGRAMED TRAINING

Several by-products which we have gained from our initial efforts in programed training I believe will be gained by any industry which trains in this way. Because the course content must be so thoroughly analyzed before it can be programed, frequently we find that the content of an already existing piece of training material can be taught best in the conventional method but in far less time than is currently the case. When we discover that the material is not suited to programing, we can then go back and more easily write an up-to-date, current, and valid lesson which can be taught much more expeditiously.

It is often difficult to tell an instructor or supervisor that he is not doing an adequate job or to point out specific weak spots in the organization of his material. However, when a student somehow lets the instructor know that he is not teaching exactly the information that he, the student, should be receiving, the instructor then on his own initiative feels obliged to familiarize himself more thoroughly with the course content. When students who have taken a programed course go back to their jobs with new facts and information which the instructor or supervisor should previously have provided but did not, this instructor or supervisor has a quick awakening, and he immediately begins studying the material himself. The result is far better on-the-job training, supervision, and rapport.

There is an amazing increase in employee morale as a result of learning by the programed format. Learning is suddenly more enjoyable and more interesting, and immediate reinforcement for the employee works wonders.

The future—I repeat—is bright, and we intend to keep current with progress as it is made. As our own studies are completed, we will submit them for publication in appropriate journals so that everyone may benefit from our efforts. Cooperation is certainly necessary and beneficial to all concerned. The present state of the art is whatever it is only because of what it is going to be and because of what it has been; it is, in a word, transitional. It behooves all of us to insure that the future *is* bright.

Lever Brothers Company

Lessons in Applying Programed Instruction to Industrial Training

By J. MYRON JOHNSON

Innovation, change, and a constant search for new ways to solve the problems of our rapidly growing industrial society are the hallmarks of our times. This is especially true for companies in the consumer products field in general and for Lever Brothers Company in particular. Lever's efforts are most readily apparent in new-product introductions. Some 60 per cent of our business is in products which did not even exist six years ago! This type of activity naturally requires a high degree of sales efficiency. Consequently, much time and effort have also been devoted to a search for new methods of improving the efficiency and effectiveness of our various training programs. Lever's decision, therefore, to make a thorough investigation of programed instruction quite early in its development is a natural outcome of the company's basic philosophy and activities.

Our interest in programed learning began with the now famous article, "Teaching Machines," by Dr. B. F. Skinner in *Science* magazine for October 1958. Since that time we have developed internally a program of 3,000-odd frames, for the indoctrination training of new salesmen, which is now being tested in the field. We also have investigated and tried out a variety of commercially produced programs.

Although a chronological, step-by-step description of our own

J. MYRON JOHNSON is Management Placement Counselor, Lever Brothers Company, New York City.

program might have some historical value, it would be limited in its educational value to others who are contemplating the use of programed instruction in their own businesses. A better approach seems to be to address ourselves to the key questions facing anyone considering programed learning and to draw on Lever's experience for at least part of the answers.

Our approach, therefore, will be to look into such questions as these: What kind of material can be programed? Who should write the program? What programing technique is applicable? What presentation methods might be used? How does one introduce programed instruction into the current training program? Following these general considerations specific illustrations based on Lever's experience will be described. It is hoped, thereby, that readers will be better able to see applications to their own problems than if we were to describe the development of a specific sales training program in the grocery industry.

What Types of Material Should Be Programed?

Certainly the first question a training manager faces is what areas programed instruction will be appropriate in. Although parts of his current training material probably can be "converted," no one has yet claimed that programed instruction can be applied to all phases of industrial training.

Three factors should be weighed in deciding whether a company should develop its own programs. Obviously it should first find out whether a similar program may not already be available or about to become available through commercial sources or from other companies working in the same area. Lists of commercially available programs can generally be obtained from any of the several publications devoted exclusively to programed instruction and from the program-publishing houses themselves. Discovering what other companies are doing is somewhat more difficult, but there has been some talk of a "clearinghouse" for programed instruction developed within companies.

It now seems likely that where subject matter might have broad implications across industry lines ("Business Letter Writing," "How to Read a Micrometer," "Business Math"), commercial firms will soon find it profitable to develop a fairly extensive number of programs. Unique training subjects peculiar to specific companies and industries, however, will have to be developed by the companies themselves. In our case it seemed highly unlikely that a commercial organization would in the foreseeable future develop programs specifically for selling in the grocery industry. Lever, therefore, elected to write its own.

The second factor to be considered is whether the subject matter can readily be programed. The majority of courses written so far have been concerned with a "conformative" type of learning, emphasizing highly factual information such as mathematics, spelling, and languages. Very little has been attempted in the so-called creative-learning areas such as creative writing or musical composition. The highly factual, non-controversial type of subject matter is far more conducive to good programing and seems to be the best place to start.

In Lever's case we have programed such subject matter as "Product Knowledge," "Company Organization," "How to Complete Sales Forms," and "Technical Jargon in the Grocery Industry." We have not yet attempted to write a program for such topics as "Closing the Sale" or "The Art of Creative Merchandising."

The final consideration is one of pure economics. The initial investment in programed instruction is quite expensive. To keep the cost per pupil to a practical level, fairly large numbers of trainees must be able to use the course. Some people have said that no fewer than 100 people should take a course to make it worthwhile, but no such arbitrary minimum can be applied consistently.

The physical location and availability of the trainees must also be considered. If, for example, an instructor could train 30 men at one time, an investment in a programed course might not be economically feasible. If, however, he had to train the 30 men individually, requiring 30 times as much instruction time, the programed course might suddenly become very attractive. In Lever's case sales training is primarily individual tutoring, and the cost of instructors is quite high.

Another economic consideration is the importance of the subject matter. Some material, which is very easily and cheaply put into a training manual, may not be worth the expense of programing. For example, Lever's company history, which is included in the older training manual, was not programed because we felt that a highly detailed knowledge of company history was not of great importance to successful job performance. It is provided in a special non-programed supplement.

One final economic consideration is the stability of the course's content. If material changes frequently—as do, for example, price lists and territorial outlines—programing it will probably prove to be uneconomical.

Who Should Program?

Once it has chosen the subject matter, a company must decide on program writers or programers. Basically, the decision is whether to program inside the company by training the current staff, to hire a programer from the outside, or to call in an outside consultant.

A major problem is the serious shortage of trained programers. Another is that training programers is not a simple matter, for not everybody makes a good one. The characteristics of a good programer are still the subject of much debate. About the only point of common agreement seems to be that the best are intensely interested in education and, by some reports, all interested in jazz! Much obviously still needs to be learned about the nature of successful programers.

Lever chose to call in a consultant, mainly because we were not willing to make the long-term investment that an addition to the staff would have meant. If a demand for programs should develop within the company, it is entirely possible that it would become economically sound to add a programer to the staff. Even so, a certain backlog of demand would have to be built up before an addition could be justified.

In programing the material used in training new salesmen, Lever used a team comprising a staff subject-matter specialist, a programer, and a staff psychologist. In view of the rapid advances being made in this area through research, the psychologist's contribution was mainly to keep the program as up to date as possible. Once the basic principles were established and the actual writing and trying out of programs began, his role sharply diminished.

The staff subject-matter specialist found it necessary to spend a great deal of time with the programer throughout the project. Although the specialist's main function is to define the training objectives as specified in a "terminal repertoire," he also has a highly important editorial and control function. He holds the final responsibility for reviewing and approving all the frames on the basis of their truth, accuracy, and clarity. In a sales-training program this responsibility cannot be overemphasized.

In the future it seems inevitable that a subject-matter specialist and a programer will be required in almost every instance. The role of the staff psychologist will undoubtedly diminish further as the technique becomes refined. For the time being, however, it seems wise to have one available for consultation in the initial planning of a program to take advantage of all the latest thinking concerning programed instruction.

What Programing Technique Should Be Used?

Much has been said recently about the so-called controversy between the Skinnerian and Crowderian techniques of programing. It seems wise not to become too closely identified with the one side or the other.

As research results build up, both approaches will undoubtedly be modified considerably, and the differences between them will be greatly reduced. In the long run laboratory results will point out the best way to program.

In the meantime, industrial users are faced with the very practical problem of selecting an approach to suit their immediate needs. Whatever the final choice may be—Crowderian or Skinnerian—it seems wise to be as flexible as possible in the beginning. The type of material to be learned will probably be the deciding factor.

Recall learning seems better handled with a Skinnerian or linear-programing approach. Recognition learning seems better handled by the multiple-choice Crowderian technique. It does not seem desirable to complicate the issue overmuch, for some types of training problems do not need elaborate devices and programs. For example, simple memorizing of paired associates might best be done by flash cards. We are seriously considering teaching price lists by brand and pack with simple cards of this type.

Lever programs are of the linear, small-step variety because the material to be learned demands recall far more than recognition. Partly, too, there was some hesitation on Lever's part to make the large investment in the mechanical equipment required in most branching courses. Finally, we were somewhat more impressed by the logical arguments behind the Skinnerian theory as opposed to those of Crowder's advocates. We remain open-minded, nevertheless, awaiting additional research results.

WHICH ARE BETTER—MACHINES OR TEXTS?

The "teaching machine" vogue has dimmed somewhat, and the programed text is gaining in popularity. Which is it better to use? Each has its advantages and disadvantages.

The big advantages of programed texts appear to be that they are cheaper to produce in small quantities and are portable. On the other hand, particularly when the program is first being built up, the text version tends to be very inflexible. It is difficult to add items or to revise them without tearing the whole book apart. Moreover, some of the programs now being devised are quite lengthy—for example, the Lever program of 3,000 frames. Finally, to write in the books themselves is much too costly because then the books cannot be used again, and to use a separate answer tape is bound to seem a bit cumbersome.

It is difficult to make flat statements about mechanical presentation devices, or teaching machines, since there is such a large variety of them, each with its own advantages and disadvantages. In general, they appear to be more flexible than texts, to be less expensive to operate when fairly large numbers of people are being trained, and to have some particularly exciting prospects for future development.

The major disadvantages in our experience have involved mechanical repair and servicing, both of which should diminish in importance as time goes on. Many machines are not portable, which limits their usefulness somewhat. Another disadvantage is that the commercially available programs come in varied sizes and styles and require considerable adaptation, with concomitant expense, to make them usable in a particular device. Perhaps some day these devices will be standardized so that all types of programs can be used in them, but that day seems to be quite distant.

Lever is currently experimenting with a text version and with two different types of mechanical devices, one using a paper roll, the other microfilm. No final conclusions have yet been drawn.

Although preliminary studies have indicated that no differences in efficiency of learning could be detected between texts and mechanical devices, the final results may not yet be in. There have been several reports that trainees may prefer a mechanical device over the long run. It is much too premature to count out the mechanical devices.

How Do You Introduce Programed Instruction?

When people hear of programed instruction or teaching machines for the first time, their almost universal reaction varies between incredulity and skepticism. Most, with further explanation and understanding, develop an overenthusiastic approval, and this is finally replaced by a certain hard-nosed yet still optimistic acceptance of new possibilities.

As with any innovation, one must anticipate encountering a natural reluctance to change. It seems pointless (and naïve) to strengthen this resistance by talking of revolutionary changes in training methods. Because of the complexity of the many concepts, a great deal of patience and forbearance is needed in explaining programed instruction to others. Indeed, the very explanation should be "programed"—the technique should sell itself. The enthusiastic claims of a new devotee are neither necessary nor desirable.

At Lever, programed instruction was presented to the field training managers with no more "sell" than was required to hold attention. The main vehicle for introducing the project was a programed filmstrip, tailor-made for Lever's use by our consultants. The field trainers were given an opportunity to ask all the questions they felt necessary and to take the programed courses themselves. They were encouraged to retain a healthy skepticism and to offer constructive criticism about the approach and about the courses. In general, their response was quite positive, but it was also tempered by a shrewdly critical reserve.

How Do You Prepare the Instructors
For Programed Instruction?

Programed instruction has a profound and dramatic effect on industrial training. Although it is highly unlikely that large numbers of instructors will suddenly become technologically unemployed, in either industry or education, some deep-seated changes in thinking and attitudes will be required on their part if this approach does receive widespread acceptance.

The problem is mainly one of integrating personal with mechanical instruction. Programed instruction tends to take over all the routine, repetitive training, leaving the more creative aspects of teaching to the instructor. Thus instructors who are merely good drillmasters are most easily replaced by programs. Neither a textbook nor a mechanical presentation device, however, can really motivate a trainee to learn. Proper motivation of the trainee therefore becomes one of the biggest, and perhaps most difficult, jobs of the instructor. Moreover, there will be a great deal of material in all training programs which will be very difficult, if not impossible, to program. The instructor won't be replaced, but his job will change.

At Lever it was necessary to revise the entire training guide for the new salesman. Subjects to be taught by programed material were clearly differentiated from those to be retained by the trainer. Great emphasis was placed on the importance of the instructor as the source of motivation for the new trainee.

The sales instructors themselves were introduced to an entirely new concept of training; their own training efforts were carefully programed in keeping with the approach we had adopted. Thus each stage of a man's learning process is carefully watched and controlled so that he is not introduced to new job material until he has completely mastered previous topics. Although this temporarily slows down the speed with which the man develops into his job, it is anticipated that time will be saved in the long run. This slowdown is quite an adjustment for many seasoned trainers to make and requires a major break with old habits. Again, it is too early to verify the effectiveness of the approach; however, the preliminary reports are encouraging.

How Do You Evaluate the Results?

More than ever before there is concern for evaluating the effectiveness of training techniques. Programed learning appears to lend itself very readily to measurement; therefore, many people expect hard and clear differences between this technique and others. That such results have not yet been forthcoming, however, is not really too surprising. Not the least stumbling block is the lack of clear-cut criteria of effectiveness for the traditional training approaches.

In measuring results we can concentrate either on the retention of programed material or on actual job performance. Retention tests are the most easily constructed but unfortunately leave unanswered the major question whether trainees can actually apply this learning to practical job problems.

In Lever's case the ultimate question is whether a technique will help "sell soap." The criteria we have developed are consequently designed to determine what effect programed instruction will have on actual job performance. As previously mentioned, programed instruction accounts for only part of a man's training, and a number of other variables must be considered, such as the differing skills of individual trainers, market conditions, and the "Hawthorne effect."

To complicate the problem further, one unexpected benefit of building our programed courses was that it revealed a number of weaknesses and omissions in our traditional training program. As a result, the programed courses contain 20 per cent more material than the training manuals. To be entirely fair, we would have to rewrite the traditional manuals to include the additional 20 per cent before making comparisons, which does not appear practical. Therefore, we anticipate that our results are unlikely to be as clear-cut as we would hope. Even so, evaluation is highly desirable not only to estimate the effectiveness of programed instruction but to suggest areas for improvement.

General Comments

Several other appropriate comments come to mind which may be of value to those considering programed instruction. Should an outside consultant be called in to write the program, it would seem highly desirable to agree in advance upon acceptable standards for the course, including agreement on a maximum error ratio per frame and the composition of an adequate test sample. In our case we settled on an average error of no more than 5 per cent per course, and no frame was to have more than 10 per cent. The sample group consisted of at least 30 preselected college students who were as evenly matched as possible with a group of Lever salesmen trainees. In addition, it was agreed that all copyrights would clearly be the property of Lever.

We discovered that programed instruction brings out a course's content in very bold relief; what one is trying to teach becomes extremely apparent. As a result, we found that some material, such as procedures or technical information which had never before been challenged in the traditional manual or lecture form, suddenly became controversial. In such instances the subject-matter specialist may have to call in company authorities from other divisions as well as from his own before a final decision can be made. The resulting improvement in the accuracy and clarity of the program will definitely be worth the extra effort.

We did purchase a few stock programs from publishers and other suppliers, some of which turned out later to be rather poor material. Fortunately, the investment in them was quite small. Those considering the purchase of commercial programs should exercise caution and demand some evidence of the courses' effectiveness.

It is obviously premature to pass final judgment on the value and future of programed instruction in industry in general and Lever Brothers in particular. It is difficult, however, to suppress one's optimism. The impact on our own training has already had some positive benefits. The experience gained in building the terminal repertoire of course objectives has had a noticeable effect on our thinking about all other aspects of training, from instruction in skilled trades to management development projects. There has also been a noticeable increase in our awareness of the need to consider basic learning principles in selecting the appropriate training techniques to achieve specific training objectives. For example, if a high degree of recall of information is required, the standard lecture method is far less likely to succeed. In such a case a programed course may be the answer.

Although a blanket recommendation cannot be given to programed-instruction techniques as being suited to all types of training situations, anyone concerned with industrial training would be well advised to pay close attention to developments in this field. As is always true with something as new as this, there is a certain risk in deciding to use it. But information is now becoming available which promises to reduce this risk considerably, and in view of the potentially handsome rewards that programed instruction promises in reduced training time and costs, the gamble might well be worthwhile.

THE PILOT STAGE

Today's sophisticated training men know that new techniques must be patiently evaluated in comparison with the old before a true measure of their effectiveness can be arrived at. This may take months or even years. Some early applications of programed instruction have, however, reached a point where preliminary findings can be shared.

Early Company Experiences In Programed Instruction

By J. L. HUGHES

The following story is told about Dr. B. F. Skinner, who is one of the pioneers in the development of teaching machines. One day, after teaching a class at Harvard, he returned to his home in Cambridge. Upon opening the front door, he happened to hear his maid say over the telephone, "Yes, that's right. Dr. Skinner is a doctor, but he's not the kind of doctor that does anybody any good." I think we will agree, however, that his maid was wrong. Dr. Skinner has made contributions to learning theory and education which promise to do many people some good.

PLANNING OF RESEARCH PROJECT

It was Dr. Skinner's publications on teaching machines that first attracted our attention at IBM. As a result, our Applied Personnel Research staff began in 1959 to consider seriously the possible use of programed instruction as a means of facilitating employee and customer training. As many people know from first-hand experience, our company engages in an extensive educational program for the training of company personnel and customers in the use of our equipment. Owing to the continual development of new products of increasing complexity, this training activity has been growing

J. L. HUGHES is Consultant, Educational Research, with IBM's Office of the Director of Education, White Plains, New York.

steadily. For this reason, we are always on the lookout for any promising new method of instruction.

An exploratory research project was therefore proposed in early 1960 in order to investigate the feasibility of applying programed instruction to our company's training program. The project called for the study of the problems associated with the training of company personnel as program writers and the writing of programs for selected company courses. It was also proposed that experiments be designed to compare quantitatively the effectiveness of programed instruction and conventional company instructional procedures in terms of class presentation time, learning achievement, and student acceptance. In the event that these initial studies turned out to be successful, it was anticipated that additional studies would be carried out in an attempt to isolate the significant variables involved and to improve the efficiency of the programed-instruction technique.

This research proposal was presented by the Applied Personnel Research group of the Corporate Staff during a meeting with representatives of our operating divisions in January 1960. After some discussion, it was agreed that the operating divisions would furnish instructors with technical knowledge in various equipment areas, and that Applied Personnel Research would train these men in programed-instruction techniques, review the programs written, and carry out studies evaluating the effectiveness of these programs. As a result, three program writers were assigned to the project to program three different maintenance engineering courses. These three courses covered the 7070 Data Processing System, the 83 Sorter, and the SAGE Computer. With the help of Dr. Robert Glaser of the University of Pittsburgh and Dr. David Klaus of the American Institute for Research as consultants on the project, the training of the program writers was begun in March 1960, and the writing and review of programs was started during the following month by three teams, each of which included one program writer and myself.

DESCRIPTION OF PROGRAMS

Let me take a moment to describe these three programs. They were all linear, straight-line programs requiring constructed responses and were prepared in programed-textbook form. The 7070 program was designed to cover the first 15 hours of lecture-discussion in a 16-week course given to maintenance engineers. The subject-matter content included the names and functions of the units of the 7070 system, bit coding, the use of data and instruction words, and the program step. This program was completed in September 1960 and consisted of 719 frames. The second program, for the 083 Sorter, was intended to replace a lecture-discussion period of six and a quarter hours in a maintenance engineering course. The subjects covered included operating controls, operating and sorting principles, circuits, and diagnostic techniques. This program, which comprised 350 frames, was completed in October. The third program, for the SAGE Computer, was designed to replace the first 18 hours of lecture-discussion in another maintenance engineering course. This material covered the basic arithmetic and logical programing instructions for the computer, address modification, the names and functions of units of the computer, and data flow. When this program was finished in January 1961, it consisted of 860 frames.

RATE OF PROGRAM PRODUCTION

One of the objects of our study was to estimate the amount of time required to prepare programs in an industrial situation. This was difficult to do, because the program writers were occasionally assigned to other duties, such as teaching, during the period in which the programs were being written. After deducting the time lost on other assignments, however, it was found that the over-all rate of program preparation was approximately 100 frames per month per man. It was also found that there were substantial variations in the rate of program preparation among the three program writers. The fastest writer was able to turn out frames at approximately twice the speed of the slowest. The differences in speed of program preparation were due to several factors, among them the differences in program-writing ability among the three men and also the relative difficulty of the subject matter that was programed. Another factor noted was the significant increase in program-writing speed as the program writers gained in experience over the first few months. It was estimated that, by the end of the third month, the program writers were able to double their writing speed.

It may be interesting for a moment to compare the rates of program production which we obtained with those reported by other investigators. A number of experienced program writers, when surveyed on the time it takes them to prepare programs, have indicated rates ranging from one to two frames per hour. This works out to approximately 175 to 350 frames per month, a higher estimated rate of production than the 100 frames per month found in our study. The reason is probably that our estimate includes all aspects of completing a program, such as writing, reviewing, rewriting, tryouts with students, preparation of artwork, typing, and reproduction. It also includes an initial period of training and organization for the project. It should be remembered that the speed of our program writing increased as the program writers gained more experience during the first few months. Toward the end of the program-writing period, they were actually producing frames at a higher rate than 100 frames per month. In view of these considerations, it appears that the frame-production estimate of 175 to 350 frames per month is closer to a true estimate for experienced program writers. Of course, it should be kept in mind that the speed of program writing is also affected by the individual differences in program-writing ability and the nature of the subject matter programed which were mentioned previously. I would like to add, parenthetically, that in subsequent efforts to train program writers our rate of frame production has reached at least 200 frames per month by the end of the first month.

DESCRIPTION OF 7070 STUDY

With our programs written, the next step in the study called for experimentation with these programs on trainees at various company training centers. Because the 7070 Data Processing System program was completed first, the initial study took place at our 7070 training center at Poughkeepsie, New York. It will be recalled that the 7070 program consisted of 719 frames which were prepared to cover the first 15-hour section of a 16-week course for maintenance engineers on the 7070 Computer. The program was presented to the trainees in five programed textbooks. Six classes totaling 70 trainees were instructed solely by means of these programed texts, which were substituted for class lectures and discussions. The instructor was present in the classroom only for the purpose of passing out the programed instruction materials and recording the time needed to complete them. He was directed to answer any questions as briefly as possible and to keep a record of all questions asked. All other aspects of the course remained unchanged. The performance of these experimental classes was compared with that of two control classes totaling 42 trainees who were taught by the lecture-discussion method customarily used at the training center.

REDUCTION IN PRESENTATION TIME

The results of this study indicated that substantial savings in presentation time and increased learning achievements were possible from the use of programed texts. While the two control classes required 15 hours over a four-day period using the conventional classroom lecture method to cover the subject matter, the six experimental classes covered it in 11 hours over a three-day period, a saving of four hours—or 27 per cent of the original training period. In later studies at the training center, it was found that even greater reductions in training time were possible using programed instruction. In ten succeeding training classes totaling 140 trainees, the classroom time allotted for programed texts was reduced to eight hours, a saving of seven hours—or 47 per cent of the original classroom presentation time of 15 hours. This was accomplished with the same improvement in learning achievement as before. The use of programed instruction thus resulted in a significant reduction in classroom presentation time when compared with conventional classroom instruction.

INDIVIDUAL DIFFERENCES AMONG TRAINEES

Another important factor affecting training time is that each trainee works individually on programed instruction. The time spent in learning these materials thus varies with each trainee, and it has been found that the slowest trainee may take more than twice as long to complete a program as the fastest one. In the initial 7070 study, although the amount of classroom time originally allotted for programed instruction was 11 hours, the time that the trainees actually took to complete the materials varied considerably from this figure. Individual differences in estimated completion time ranged from 7.2 to 15.3 hours, and the average completion time was 9.8 hours. Some students were therefore able to review the material studied in class, while others had to spend additional time outside of class to learn this material. Since homework has always been required in these courses, the same condition prevailed in the control classes.

There are thus considerable differences among trainees in the time they take to complete programs. This gives rise to the problem of what to do with the trainee who finishes early. While this may seem to pose administrative difficulties, problems of this sort should actually be welcomed. The variation in pace among the trainees is one of the main advantages of programed instruction. The brighter trainees can proceed more quickly through the material without becoming bored by the more plodding pace frequently found in classroom instruction and can quickly complete the basic course requirements. The slower trainees, on the other hand, can take the additional time they need to understand the subject and acquire a sound grasp of its fundamentals. In the meantime, the brighter trainees can be put to work on advanced programed instruction, laboratory problems, or other supplementary learning materials. Or, if they are studying the material in a decentralized location, such as a company office or plant, rather than in a large company training center, they can return to productive work sooner. It is the latter possibility which makes programed instruction particularly promising for industrial training.

IMPROVEMENT IN LEARNING

In addition to reducing training time, another potential advantage of using programed instruction in industry is that it can result in trainees' learning a subject more thoroughly. In the 7070 training experiment, it was found that the average score of the programed-instruction classes on a comprehensive, two-hour achievement test was nine points higher than that for the control classes, with the experimental group averaging 95 compared to 86 for the control group. What was particularly striking was the reduced distribution of scores for the experimental classes. Only 11 per cent of the experimental group scored below 90 on the test, compared to 57 per cent below 90 for the control group. Apparently more trainees in the experimental group really mastered the subject matter as measured by the criterion of the achievement test.

TRAINEE ATTITUDE

Another variable which we measured in this study was trainee reaction to exposure to the new method. Obviously, this is a very important factor in considering the adoption of a new method of training. Therefore, an attitude questionnaire was constructed and administered anonymously to the experimental group. The results indicated that the trainees were generally very favorable toward programed instruction. Of the group, 87 per cent liked programed instruction better than the conventional instruction which they had experienced in other company courses, and 83 per cent indicated that they would prefer using it in place of the customary lecture-discussion method. Only 6 per cent liked programed instruction less than conventional instruction, and 13 per cent indicated that they would have some objections to using it in future courses. The amount of dissatisfaction with programed instruction was thus found to be very low. Student comments were generally enthusiastic and indicated a realization of the ease and efficiency of this new method of teaching. A content analysis of comments made by the trainees indicated that the most frequently liked aspects of programed instruction were its effectiveness as a method of instruction and the trainee's ability to proceed at his own individual rate. Certain characteristics of the method itself were also favorably commented on, such as the repetition of important points, the gradual and logical sequence of presentation, and the way it maintained the trainee's attention and concentration.

Some aspects of programed instruction, however, were mentioned unfavorably by a few trainees. Most of these comments related to the mechanical features of the method, such as the repetition of responses required and the need to turn pages constantly. Other comments referred to the desirability of interspersing periods of programed instruction with other training techniques and providing for discussion periods with an instructor. Anyone interested in applying programed instruction to industrial training would do well to heed these comments in planning the use of programed instruction in his organization. It was interesting to note, however, that none of these negative comments was made by more than 10 per cent of the trainees. Further, a number of aspects of programed instruction which were unfavorably commented on in the original study have been subsequently eliminated by improvements in the programed-textbook format. In the initial study, for example, the trainee would read a frame in the programed text, write in his response, and turn the page for reinforcement of his response. He then had to turn another page to read the next frame. In the preparation of programed texts for later studies, answers to frames were printed on the back of the presentation frame so that the trainee had only to turn the page once to check his response and read the next presentation frame, thereby cutting down the page turning by half. This was accomplished without any reduction in learning achievement.

LATER STUDIES

As indicated before, later studies of programed instruction in ten succeeding 7070 training classes totaling 140 trainees at the same training center have confirmed the results of the first study. Thus a total of 252 trainees were involved in these studies, which were conducted over a nine-month period. In addition, studies have been completed during the past year at another company training center using the 083 Sorter program to teach the maintenance of this machine. These have also indicated the advantage of programed instruction over conventional instruction. For example, the average achievement test score of eight classes totaling 150 trainees who used programed instruction was 87. For three classes totaling 57 trainees who used the lecture-discussion method, the average test score was 81. There was thus a gain of six points in achievement for the classes who used programed instruction. The results of these repeated industrial studies indicate the significant improvement in training efficiency that is possible from the use of programed instruction.

In addition to these comparative studies, we have also conducted research on the effect of changes in programed texts which were designed to make them more efficient. The first change called for the students to write their answers on a separate answer pad rather than in the programed textbook itself. This would permit the programed textbooks to be used over and over again on a number of students, and would reduce the number of texts required. A second change, which was mentioned earlier, was to print the reinforcement or correct answer on the back of the page containing the original frame rather than on the succeeding page as in the original format for the programed text. If the reinforcement could be printed on the back of the page in this fashion, the next frame could be printed on the succeeding page, thereby reducing by half the amount of page turning by the trainee. The results for classes in which these changes in program-text format were introduced indicated that there were no significant differences in learning achievement under these conditions.

Another study sought to determine the effect on learning achievement of not having students write their answers to the frames of the program. This is known as "covert responding" in contrast to "overt responding" or writing the answers. It was found that the omission of written responses by trainees produced no effect on their achievement test scores, a finding which has also been reported by other investigators. Thus overt responding in the form of written answers by the trainee does not appear to be a significant factor in the immediate retention of programed instruction material. If this is also true of retention for a longer period of time, the finding obviously has some important implications. If much of the written response to programs can be eliminated, the trainee can complete the program more quickly. One of his main sources of dissatisfaction with programs, the repetition in writing of similar responses, is also removed.

PLANS FOR FUTURE

As a result of positive research findings on the use of programed instruction in our training programs, our company has been expanding its efforts in this area. We plan to continue research on manipulating different variables to improve the efficiency of present programed-instruction methods in the industrial training situation. In addition, program-writing staffs have been set up in the operating divisions in order to prepare programs for the courses given by these divisions. A number of additional programs have already been prepared in subjects ranging from the maintenance of equipment to Boolean algebra. It is contemplated that much of the instruction on computers and computer programing can be carried out by programed instruction. Other areas of application, such as clerical, sales, and management training, will also be investigated. In addition to training employees, it is further anticipated that the programed-instruction method will be extended to customer training. Experimental programs have already been developed in the basic accounting machine area, and these are currently being tested.

The 7070 Data Processing System program, which was the subject of much experimentation at our Poughkeepsie training center, has now been expanded from the original 719 frames to 1,320 frames. The next stage of this research project calls for sending this material out to branch offices in a complete training package consisting of the 7070 program, a TV kinescope explaining its use, and an achievement test for use by the local manager. It is anticipated that, by decentralizing this training, at least three days of instruction formerly given at a company training center can now be given at the local branch office. The use of this material is currently being tested and evaluated. If successful, it will demonstrate the feasibility of using programed instruction for decentralized training with its attendant reduction of training costs to the company.

❊   ❊   ❊

This briefly describes some of our activity in the programed-instruction area. Our initial efforts have been encouraging, and we intend to continue our investigations. We hope by this means to contribute to a greater understanding of this new training technique and to broaden its applications to industrial training.

Sandia Corporation

Programed Self-Instructional Materials in Background Courses

By ROBERT F. UTTER

The Sandia Corporation of Albuquerque, New Mexico, is a primary contractor to the Atomic Energy Commission. It employs approximately 8,000 people and maintains an extensive educational and training program. From September 1960 to September 1961, 2,590 employees were enrolled for out-of-hours courses, with 1,649 completions; more than 2,000 enrolled for in-hours courses, with 1,590 completions; and 72 young engineers (principally) enrolled in educational development courses at the University of New Mexico. Most of the trades courses were given to meet the needs of two apprenticeship courses: machinist and electronics.

Three TMI-Grolier programed self-instruction courses were offered at Sandia during the same period. The total enrollment for the three courses was 279, with 208 completions; the ratio of completions to enrollment was 74.5 per cent.

Russian was the most popular offering. Five classes were conducted in the subject; the total enrollment was 158, with 121 completions, giving a 77.2 per cent completion ratio. "Algebra I" was given to build the background of students who could not qualify for entrance into college algebra classes. A total of 87 students enrolled in algebra and 62 completed the course, resulting in a 71.2 per cent completion ratio. "Descriptive Statistics" was taken by 34 students, 25 of whom finished the course for a completion ratio of 73.5 per cent.

ROBERT F. UTTER is with Sandia's Technical & Trades Training Division, Sandia Base, Albuquerque, New Mexico.

There were four principal motivating reasons for adopting the programed self-instruction method of teaching:

1. The corporation wanted to keep abreast of new developments in training methods.
2. It wanted to reduce the cost per pupil for the instruction of small classes—especially apprenticeship classes, which generally are small.
3. It wanted to improve the quality of instruction in small classes.
4. It wanted to give more individual instruction in the larger classes, especially in the fundamentals of certain subjects such as electronics, algebra, geometry, Russian, and so on.

The opinions of the courses expressed by both students and instructors were favorable. Students liked the idea of working at their own pace, while instructors felt that they were doing more effective work since they concentrated on individual problems as they arose. Instructors and students also liked the elimination of make-up work for absentees.

In general, Sandia is pleased with the results achieved by using programed instructional materials. We were especially impressed to learn that the percentage of completions for the programed courses was higher than that for conventional classes in the same subjects: 74.5 per cent as against 64.0 per cent.

MAJOR FINDINGS IN FIVE PROGRAMS USED

To summarize briefly the large body of material reported to management, I can only outline the major findings in five programs, including those I have already mentioned, that we have used at the Sandia Corporation.

TMI "Descriptive Statistics." The first program was an experiment which the Personnel Department conducted, using the Teaching Machines, Inc. course in "Descriptive Statistics." Twenty-five students agreed to take the "Descriptive Statistics" program purely on a self-study basis, with a pre-test and a post-test to show their gain in knowledge of the statistical material covered by the program. With no scheduled classes and no particular pressure for completion, seven persons failed to complete the program. Four took fewer than 20 working hours to complete it. In general, the group taking between 20 and 30 hours of work time to complete the program scored the greatest gains on the post-test.

From this trial run we learned several things: First, end-of-chapter quizzes definitely should be inserted into the program in order to evaluate student progress as well as to provide for self-evaluation. Secondly, it was very clear that additional problems were needed as homework assignments to give the students a larger context in which to work; that is, the frame size in the program was too limited to permit a student to manipulate all of the elements necessary to apply his knowledge to a practical problem. In general, the students learned the materials covered by the program reasonably well, but there was evidence of lack of ability to extrapolate the knowledge gained to unfamiliar situations.

TMI "Fundamentals of Algebra." The second experiment was a non-credit algebra program to prepare students who were unable to attempt a course in post-high school algebra ("Math I," technical institute level). Twelve students enrolled for the course, and all completed the program in the fall semester of 1960. They were given a pre-test on the Cooperative Algebra Test Form T and a post-test on the Cooperative Test Form Z. Student reaction to the program was highly favorable, and satisfactory gains in knowledge were made by the bulk of the group completing the course.

In a parallel "Math A" lecture course, 20 students enrolled and 14 completed the work. The major finding derived from this small group was that the content of the TMI algebra program was insufficient to review the entire field of high school algebra to prepare students satisfactorily for the post-high school course. It would, then, be necessary to develop supplemental materials to broaden the scope of the program. This has since been done.

A range of completion times was obtained, and we found that those starting on the lower end tended to gain more than those starting at a higher level. The extremely small step size produced some minor complaints of boredom from the better students; however, these complaints were not deemed sufficient to impede the usefulness of this program seriously. The main problem was covering the subject matter.

"Fundamentals of AC and DC Electricity" (*ETL Experimental*

Program). The third major study, which is still under way, has been participated in by 20 students. This is a joint experimental program with the Bell Telephone Laboratories which I am administering. The subject matter of the program is basic elements of DC and AC electricity. The program is highly sophisticated and includes a number of innovations not present in any of the commercially available programs we have seen. The primary objective of our experiment was to take a distributed-trials approach to a program which had originally been devised for a massed-learning approach. The volunteer students ranged widely in intelligence and in reading-comprehension level. In general, they knew little basic electricity prior to starting the program.

The findings are many, but here are a few highlights: An instructor who is present in the room is called on to answer very few questions by the students. The program is largely self-contained, and possibly the format tends to inhibit the students from asking questions when they experience difficulty. Second, the supplemental materials which are handed out—that is, problem sets and the like—are extremely well received by the students; this practice should definitely be continued with any future programs. Third, the illustrative diagrammatic materials included with the program are similar to textbook or instructor-prepared materials. By using large panels, it was possible to include much material which could not have been retained in small-size frames. Fourth, the looseleaf format used in these Sandia experiments has given rise to serious distribution and warehousing problems. The total bulk of material, even for a class of only 20 students, includes some 20 cartons of paper. This is going to continue to be a vexing problem. Fifth, as in most programs, analyzing student responses has been a very time-consuming occupation. Thus far, approximately 80 hours of clerical time have been devoted to putting onto Royal McBee cards the information obtained from the students' responses. We anticipate that about 30 more hours of work will be required to post all the experimental data. The cards' format will happily allow rapid analysis of the data obtained in subsequent item revision.

Preliminary analysis of student responses by subjects and by frames indicates that the program, in spite of its occasional large steps, is satisfactorily imparting complex information. It is clear that the weakest students need remedial loops to eliminate difficulties that appear fairly early in the program. The biggest difficulty encountered appears to be in the students' lack of mathematical sophistication. Although the program calls only for a background in high school algebra, some students who had this preparation nonetheless have encountered their major difficulty in its mathematical portions.

A subexperiment is being run to expose some volunteers to laboratory experience to round out the programed material, which is essentially a substitute for lectures. Thus far, the background of the students appears to be adequate, and they are encountering little difficulty in utilizing the self-instruction manuals customarily used in the laboratory as well as some simple electrical gear. Motivation is lagging, however, and future work will require more advanced preparation to integrate the lab exercises and the program.

Another important finding is that the conceptual organization of the program is sound. The results of unit-mastery tests at the end of each major learning block indicate a reasonable level of learning. On only a few occasions have we observed a person apparently putting his mental gears in neutral and going through a sizable number of frames without comprehension or retention of the material he has covered. One student with extremely rapid reading speed went through portions of the program entirely too quickly for proper assimilation.

Although all the figures are not yet in, it appears that spaced learning slows down a student in learning material designed for a two-week learning period.

"Math A," Spring 1961. A very large number of students—74, to be exact—enrolled in two sections of a make-up mathematics course, again using the TMI algebra program. Thus far the results appear to be about the same as those of the smaller pilot groups, and we will soon have test data to evaluate the effectiveness of the program. Some lectures have been added to supplement the program. Its limitations have yet to be overcome, and we are looking forward to receiving the second volume from TMI. This should provide the necessary programed self-instructional materials to enable the supplement to be handled without lectures.

TMI "Basic Russian." One of the newest and apparently most successful programs is the introduction to the Russian language, another TMI program. A class of 48 students divided into two sections is learning the Cyrillic alphabet, a limited Russian vocabulary, and some of the basic grammatical rules. There are a number of novel features about the program, including the special phonetic alphabet or pronunciation system developed to teach Russian words. Students in the class have been disappointed at the lack of practice in pronunciation, and the program has been supplemented by the instructor to provide some training in pronouncing Russian words. The completion rate for the course—that is, the lack of drop-outs —is highly gratifying. In the previous lecture-type introductory Russian course the drop-out rate was heavy. The students currently completing the course probably will not have developed very much skill, but a substantial percentage will be ready to continue at a somewhat intermediate level between the normal first course and the start of the second course.

The program does not include any formal presentation of conjugated Russian verbs. The instructor, however, assembled as hand-out material some of the verbs included in the program whose conjugation had been completed but spread over a variety of frames. The students' reaction to this supplemental material has been favorable. It appears that learning verb forms by individual frames is more successful than the classic textbook fashion of teaching all forms of the verb at the same time, but the summary or outline of this material assembled by the instructor evidently helps the student to consolidate his learning. We look for this principle to be broadly applicable in a number of programs. Most of the students in the class have inquired whether additional material will be made available so that they may study Russian further. Unfortunately, at this time we are unable to supply more advanced material in the programed format. We are thus led to recommend to these serious students what materials they should use to continue their studies. These materials will have to be in conventional textbook format, and their development will be carried out in a non-credit voluntary class.

COMPARATIVE COSTS FOR CONVENTIONAL AND
TMI PROGRAMED SELF-INSTRUCTION CLASSES

The costs of instruction in Russian at Sandia Corporation during the period of September 1, 1960, to September 1, 1961, were: (1)

for conventional classes, $571.50, or $57.15 per completion; and (2) for TMI programed classes, $2,443.50, or $20.19 per completion. This is a difference of $36.96 per completion. The costs of instruction in algebra for the same period were: (1) for conventional classes, $246.00, or $20.50 per completion; and (2) for TMI programed classes, $1,041.00, or $16.79 per completion—a difference of $3.71 per completion. These costs and the percentages of students who actually completed the courses are indicated in the following chart:

Class	Enroll-ment	Comple-tions	Cost for Instructor and Instructional Materials	Cost per Completion of Course
Russian, conventional class	60	10 (16.7%)	$571.50	$57.15
Russian, TMI class	158	121 (77.2%)	$2,443.50	$20.19
Algebra, conventional class	18	12 (66.7%)	$246.00	$20.50
Algebra, TMI class	87	62 (71.2%)	$1,041.00	$16.79

The differences in cost per completion for the two methods of instruction are due to the differences in percentage of completions. The cost of instructors' salaries for each class and the cost of teaching materials for each completion were approximately the same.

The low ratio of completions to enrollment in the conventional Russian class was a motivating factor in Sandia's adopting the TMI programed-instruction materials. Only one academically qualified instructor is available to us to teach Russian, and he is not qualified to teach the introductory course, judging by the low ratio of completions to enrollments mentioned above. He knows and speaks the language, but he will not organize a step-by-step plan of instruction for the introductory course. The use of TMI programed materials for beginners' classes which can be conducted by advanced students in Russian has filled this void in the educational program, leaving the academically qualified instructor to teach the advanced classes.

SUGGESTIONS FOR IMPROVED MATERIALS

A number of problems still exist to which we need solutions. We should, for example, learn a great deal more about sustaining the motivation of students in programed self-instruction. Although the successful completion of frames does indeed seem to have a positive motivational effect, at the moment we have serious reservations about the ability of programs to continue to provide this type of motivation. Research information concerning motivational variables would be extremely helpful.

A second important point pertains to research information about retention. In our formalized training efforts we are continuously faced with the problem of having to *assume* the student's competence, but instructors frequently find that previous material has not been adequately retained. It appears at the moment that programs may do a better job in this respect than conventional instruction, but we need positive evidence on this point.

Third, what new techniques are being developed to integrate programed self-instruction with other types of instructional material? As long as the important principle of allowing each student to proceed at his own pace continues to be incorporated into the programs —and, parenthetically, let me add that this may be their most important virtue—we are then faced with a serious problem in attempting to integrate lecture materials or other demonstrations into programs. Clearly, a teacher with 30 students is not going to repeat the same lecture ten times, even though he might be called upon to do so if each student is allowed to break or interrupt his programed material. If the program is entirely self-contained, on the other hand, it may be of such great length that it will lose its practicality in our industrial training situation where only a small proportion of a man's waking hours can be devoted to such instruction.

Recent releases of commercially available programs have given industrial training people some potentially valuable new tools. Our experience in training courses has confirmed this fact. We find, however, that the decision to try out such programs for evaluating their usefulness as parts of the over-all training effort is complicated by a paucity of descriptive and analytic materials. The following list reflects the kinds of information we need:

1. Every program package should include a lattice and/or matrix containing the major concepts in the program and their sequence of presentation. It is likely that such tools are used in developing most programs, and their inclusion should require little effort.
2. The programer should list the criteria of behavior that a learner should display upon completing a program. This would greatly assist the user, as well as provide protection for the programer.
3. The reference materials used in developing the program should be specifically cited. In order to evaluate the program initially and to fit it in with additional materials, reference data would be helpful.
4. The level of the program should be specified in more detail than by grade level. Such factors as vocabulary level, concepts assumed, or, in general, the experiential background expected of the student might serve as criteria.
5. Better estimates of time for programed-instruction study would be helpful. They would have to be reported in ranges, since the self-pacing feature is a powerful advantage of these programs. A special case we have encountered is spaced versus massed learning. Where only a few hours a week can be devoted to study, as in a conventional semester course, it appears that more working time may be required to complete a program.
6. It would be a great service if programers would provide supplemental exercises, problem sets, and summary materials (to take the place of what otherwise would be contained in the students' notes). Larger contexts than those provided by frames can be included more readily in problem sets.
7. Programs organized in a unit or chapter format are easiest to evaluate. One can insert mastery tests into such a format and thereby more readily determine student progress. In long, non-branching programs logical breakpoints could be indicated by the programer.

8. It would be highly desirable if more sophisticated and economical ways of recording and analyzing feedback could be provided. At the present time the task of analyzing student responses in non-branching programs is inordinately time-consuming. The possibility of improving programs through feedback is exciting and significant if the data-processing problems can be overcome.

9. Lastly, specifying external measures of criteria—such as standardized tests—is properly a responsibility of the programs' users. However, such criteria *will* be used, and the programer's suggestions should be on record.

Kearfott Division
General Precision, Inc.

Machine-Teaching for Company Service Personnel and Customer Trainees

By GEORGE SKROBLUS

The Kearfott Division of General Precision, Inc. develops, manufactures, and sells many types of systems, components, controls, and measuring instruments for aircraft and guided missiles. Some of these items are motors, servos, synchros, gyros, amplifiers, radio compass loops, indicators, 360° counters, and Hermeflexes. Kearfott also developed and is manufacturing the J-4 and N-1 compass systems, which are standard equipment on most aircraft. The company has pioneered in central gyro reference systems and is now one of the major producers of inertial-guidance and control equipment for the missile industry. In addition, Kearfott has expanded into areas such as microwave, electrohydraulics, and ground support equipment.

The Customer Services and Parts Division of Kearfott is responsible for caring for the product after it leaves the plant and is delivered to the customer. Besides supplying such services as writing technical manuals, provisioning tools, test equipment, and spare parts, repairing products, and supplying field service engineers all

GEORGE SKROBLUS is Supervisor, Service Training and Methods, Customer Services. Kearfott is located in Little Falls, New Jersey.

over the world, the division maintains an important Service Training Center.

The Service Training Center is responsible for the technical training of Service Division personnel and all customers—who, because
of Kearfott's product line, are mainly military people. Service Division personnel training is directed toward two major groups: our
salaried field engineer force and the hourly-paid technicians working
in our Service Repair Shop. All management training and the technical training of company personnel in the other operating divisions
are handled by other training groups.

SERVICE TRAINING CENTER COURSES

The technical-training problem facing the Service Training Center
is in most respects similar to any other technical-training problem.
The inertial-guidance field may be broken down into its technical
parts and presented piece by piece. However, one great difficulty is
that because of constant advances in the state of the art, much of the
material presented by the Training Center is not yet in textbooks.
This is particularly true of service training because we are primarily
interested in the theory of operation, trouble shooting, and repair.
Much of the design or basic-theory information contained in current
textbooks is not applicable to our needs; so we must write our own
texts.

The Service Training Center presents four types of courses, which
are described below.

Type A: Background Development. Type A courses are presented
for purposes of background development—that is, to bring the technical qualifications of our trainees up to a level at which they can
understand inertial-guidance principles. The courses cover such subjects as algebra, trigonometry, basic electronics, use of the slide rule,
theory of the oscilloscope, and the like and are important to us
because of the exceptionally varied levels of our students' previous
education and training. Until guidance systems were developed
several years ago, many of Kearfott's employees were primarily
skilled in mechanical jobs and had very little contact with systems
relying on electronic circuitry. The expansion of the company product line led to the establishment of an Electronic and Systems Division and the development of electronic fundamentals and skills in all

employees having technical contact with these complex systems. A very important job of the Service Training Center today is to prepare those of our personnel who have mechanical backgrounds for work in the field of electronics.

Type B: Basic Avionics Subjects. Our basic avionics subjects are directly applicable to our inertial-guidance systems and were extracted from the technical descriptions of those systems. They embody common requirements for most of Kearfott's products and were especially isolated for that reason. They are covered in 26 different courses on such subjects as accelerometers, Schuler tuning, Coriolis effects, earth's rate correction, principles of gyroscopes, ball-bearing handling, and so on, none of which is fully described from a maintenance point of view in commercially available textbooks. The presentation time for each of these prepared-in-house courses varies from one to twelve hours depending upon the course.

Systems Servicing. Kearfott manufactures more than 25 different systems which, at the present time, require training for their servicing. For our own service engineers, training usually starts toward the completion of the research and development phase and continues for the life of the product. Customer training usually begins after the system has gone into production; the tools and test equipment used in maintaining it have been produced by this time, too, and continue to be used throughout the life of the product. Course-presentation time varies from 40 to 320 hours, depending upon the particular system and whether a depot or field-level maintenance course is being taught.

Administrative Concepts. Courses in administrative concepts, consisting of such subjects as company organization and policies, military field operations, report writing, methods of instruction, the role of the contractor, and other corporate matters, are given only to Service Division personnel. Their presentation time varies from half an hour to four hours.

DIFFICULTIES ENCOUNTERED IN TRAINING-PROGRAM ADMINISTRATION

The ideal training situation is, of course, that which occurs when you can tightly control the entrance requirements, effectively motivate the students, assemble them all in the same place at the same time, supply them with a well-qualified instructor, have them all speaking the same language, and then have the time necessary to conduct the training. Our service-training conditions are far from this ideal.

Most of our students, particularly the military ones, display a tremendous variety of backgrounds, and their motivation for taking the courses may also vary considerably. Our own employees naturally have more motivation, but their backgrounds, too, may vary from that of the mechanical engineer or technician to that of the electrical engineer or technician. The assignments of field engineers take them all over the world, and it is very difficult to return them to our Service Training Center for training in a group. As a result, during one month the Service Training Center may have two engineers in training on one system, and the next month fourteen may be awaiting training in as many as eight different systems. The number of instructors we must plan for varies accordingly from one to eight over a very short period! This is certainly not a stable situation from either management's or the instructor's point of view.

Kearfott and its parent company, General Precision, Inc., are very active in international sales. As an example, we in the Service Training Center are faced with the problem of teaching the same course, at different times, to American, Japanese, German, Dutch, and Swedish trainees. Interpreters may have to be hired for the full duration of the training program, and time is lost while each word the instructor speaks is repeated to the class in its native tongue.

Scheduling the necessary amount of time is always a problem, and we are constantly looking for ways in which we can shorten the training period.

Although this is not commonly of major importance, we sometimes experience difficulty in obtaining competent technicians who are also skilled in the application of learning theory. It is also difficult for a training manager to supervise an instructor adequately unless he knows the subject as well as the instructor and constantly monitors the instructor's presentations until confidence in his ability has been proved justified. This is physically and economically impossible as well as insulting to the instructor. Some supervision can be exercised by monitoring the course outline, lesson plans, and examinations, by paying short visits to the classroom, and by conversing with the students; but the students' reliability is doubtful, and only vague trends may be distinguishable from their comments.

It is because of all these difficulties that the Kearfott Service Training Center has actively followed the development of teaching machines and programed instruction.

KEARFOTT'S EXPERIENCE WITH PROGRAMED INSTRUCTION

Early in 1961 the Service Training Center acquired a teaching machine for a trial period of three months. Along with the machine we obtained courses in algebra, trigonometry, basic electronics, oscilloscope theory, and use of the slide rule. The courses were presented for one hour each day, three days a week, to each of seven repair-shop supervisors. The program lasted for the full three months and is briefly summarized below. Throughout this discussion the terms "teaching machine" and "programed instruction" will be used interchangeably, but I wish to emphasize that it is the *programed instruction* that teaches and not the machine.

Findings of the Trial Period. Everyone taking the courses was favorably impressed with the program's ability to teach and is now a confirmed believer in programed instruction. The enthusiasm has spread to other departments of the division, and we are now trying to fulfill the many requests for use of the machine. The machine with its program *did* teach, and its effect was obvious to the shop superintendent in the improvement of his supervisors' technical background. One instructor was assigned full-time to monitor the program and wound up doing so on a part-time basis. He was able to continue with his regular assignments and occasionally take time to set up the machine or to tutor. Surprisingly little tutoring was required.

In many instances, one or another of the shop supervisors was delayed in attending his scheduled session, but no inconvenience resulted. The monitoring instructor was able to continue with the assignment since there was no large group of trainees sitting in the classroom, waiting for the late-comers. If we had had to, we could have moved the machine to a supervisor's desk and let him take the course without going to a classroom.

Each student was able to proceed at his own pace. For example, the course in basic electronics varied in presentation time from

5¼ to 8½ hours. The error count varied just as much, but not in direct proportion.

Current Uses and Future Plans. Since the results of the trial period were so favorable and since we recognized that the teaching machine could provide solutions to other problems, the Service Training Center recommended that Kearfott purchase the machine. Our top managers are progressive, and the appropriation was approved in a very short time. The Service Training Center has thus launched its career in programed learning.

To build a respectable library of programs as quickly as possible, we intend to subcontract the programing of some of our subjects to outside sources. Then, as our in-house programing capability develops, we will assume more of the programing tasks and rely less on outside sources. We are currently depending almost entirely upon commercially available programs.

Eventually, we intend to program most of the four types of courses mentioned above, but at present we shall concentrate on the basic avionics subjects. One of our better instructors is scheduled to attend a one-month course in programing being given by the teaching machine manufacturer early in 1962.

As this paper is being written, the teaching machine has been in use for six months, presenting Type A (background development) courses, and although it is no panacea, several advantages have become obvious. A considerable saving in the students' and the instructors' time has resulted. Instead of using an instructor to originate a course and teach it as required, we can use a less highly paid assistant instructor to monitor the machine's presentation of a program and to answer the few questions as they arise. The instructor is thereby freed to create additional programs.

Prior to their taking a training course, we pre-test the students, determine their weaknesses, and then assign separate teaching-machine programs to each. By using several machines, one instructor (or assistant instructor) can handle many different programed courses at the same time. This new capability has eliminated the impractical situation of having as many instructors as there are different courses or of conducting one instructor-presented course which is designed to *try* to cover the average needs of a large class. Such a course bores the bright students and loses the dull ones.

On a voluntary basis, the teaching machine is now also being used with our customer trainees for upgrading their technical background prior to beginning their systems training. The effects and benefits of its use in this respect have been particularly outstanding because it obviates any possible difficulties that could arise from poor student motivation and the variety of the students' entrance qualifications. The mechanical gadgetry and the effectiveness of the programs appear to have made learning easier, and directly or indirectly have increased the students' motivation. We notice that the average final examination grade in one of our systems courses has increased slightly since the application of the teaching machine.

What is the future of programed learning and teaching machines at Kearfott's Service Training Center? Our maximum effort will be exerted toward applying this new technique to our customer-training responsibility. Naturally, the training of our own personnel will benefit from the programs developed for our customers. We intend to offer our customers a choice of conventional courses, programed instruction, or both. The customer-training problem that we are most interested in solving quickly is that of the differences in language characteristic of General Precision's international customers. We intend to program those systems destined for international use and then translate them into the native tongues of our customers.

Captive Customers and Professional Students

As far as Kearfott's Service Training Center is concerned, programed learning and teaching machines are here to stay and will be heavily relied upon in the future. The field is developing rapidly—but, in our opinion, not rapidly enough because of the two closely related problems of the captive program customer and the influence of the professional student. Let me explain. Each training group that wishes to use programs and teaching machines is now held captive to the manufacturer of the particular machine chosen and can use only those programs which are developed by that manufacturer. At the present time this severely limits the number of programs that can be presented and, therefore, also limits the expansion of programed instruction.

Closely allied to this captive-customer problem is the influence of what I call "the professional student." The professional student is quick to align himself behind the leader or originator of a theory that he agrees with and to consider all other theories false. Those who believe in his theory are "saints," and those who don't are "sinners." Hence, today, in the field of programed instruction, we have the Skinnerians, the Crowderians, and the "Matheticians," each expounding the virtues of his theory.

I earnestly feel that what is needed in the programed-instruction field today is a teaching machine that will accommodate all types of programs and a cooperative attitude on the part of all the various schools of thought. All types of programing are effective, and each has its place in industrial training. What we want is perhaps a fee-and-royalty arrangement for programers which will allow a particular program to be used in several manufacturers' machines, thereby making it possible for a user's library of programs to expand and fit his own particular needs.

Plumbing and Heating Division
American-Standard

Programed Instruction in the Training of Salesmen

By E. M. CAMPBELL

At American-Standard we are constantly faced with the problem of training new salesmen, retraining and refreshing the existing sales force, and introducing new materials and/or new products. Most of our trainee-salesmen do not have engineering backgrounds, yet they are called upon not only to sell a semi-engineered product but to be able to advise and assist in its installation and service. In seeking a way to impart information in all these activities, we remind ourselves, also, that day-to-day field problems do not necessarily have definite solutions, although experience has shown that there usually is one answer that is more valid than any of the others.

At our training school and at our district meetings the facts have been presented in lectures, conferences, and examinations with strong audio-visual support, including sound-slide films and sound movies. However, in analyzing our educational results, we discovered that the following factors apparently precluded our achieving maximum benefits:

1. The differences in formal educational background which are prevalent among the students.

E. M. CAMPBELL is Manager of Sales Personnel Development for American-Standard's Plumbing and Heating Division, with headquarters in New York City.

91

2. Differing field experience, due to area of assignment and degree of specialization.
3. Student sophistication, evident from such comments as "Just another lecture!" "Just another training film!" and similarly flip remarks.

PROGRAMED INSTRUCTION BY MARK II AUTOTUTOR

When programed instruction was brought to the attention of the Sales Personnel Development Unit, teams were assigned to investigate both the Skinnerian and the Crowderian methods. Here was a new way to present both review and advanced material to tired veterans and eager trainees.

We selected the Crowderian method as most suited to our particular program with its set targets and the probability of attaining them. Crowder presents the student with multiple choices—just as do actual field problems. Crowder also requires that point one be absorbed before the student can proceed to point two, and so on. The team members who were investigating the various methods of programing instructional material, however, quickly learned how to "beat" a scrambled book, and they reasoned that the students would soon make the same discoveries. The next logical step, therefore, was to use a teaching machine.

We chose to institute a pilot program using the Mark II Auto-Tutor. Here was a patient yet stubborn teacher that presented programed instruction by means of a familiar-seeming device, for it is in appearance much like the television set with its channel-selecting buttons.

We had previously developed for use during our training sessions a short course which we called "The Six-Point Program for the Sale of Hydronic Heating." We discussed our problems, targets, future plans, and the like with members of U.S. Industries' Educational Science Division, the marketers of the AutoTutor, and they undertook to program our course and commit it to film for use in a pilot program.

The "guinea pigs" for this experiment were sales and clerical personnel from five of our East Coast sales offices: Philadelphia, New York, Newark, Long Island, and New England. One man in each

Sample Questions from Examination

1. Which one of these things is an extra source of internal heat?

The chimney	Button D
The refrigerator	Button C
A five-year-old boy	Button B
All of these are heat sources.	Button A

2. Now let's say you have calculated the heat loss for a house at 108,000 Btu/hr. Looking over the situation, you decide that the house has about the normal amount of vagrant heat producers. If this is so, about how much heat must the heating system produce?

81,000 Btu/hr	Button C
108,000 Btu/hr	Button B
144,000 Btu/hr	Button A

3. If you were engineering a heating system for this house, you would want one with a net rating of:

81,000 Btu/hr	Button D
108,000 Btu/hr	Button C
At least 120,000 Btu/hr	Button B

4. Below are some of the specifications for three of the G-2 gas-fired boilers. The gross and net capacities are given. Our house requires 108,000 Btu/hr according to the I=B=R heat loss calculation. Which boiler is appropriate?

	Btu/hr (gross)		
Boiler Number	A.G.A. Output	Net I=B=R Rating	Button
G-25	96,000	72,000	C
G-26	120,000	90,000	B
G-27	144,000	108,000	A

5. Look at the specifications for the G-26 and G-27 again. We have already determined that the G-27 would be the usual choice for our house demanding 108,000 Btu/hr. Would the G-26 boiler qualify for the economy-type installation outlined in this paragraph?

	Btu/hr (gross)	
Boiler Number	A. G. A. Output	Net I=B=R Rating
G-26	120,000	90,000
G-27	144,000	108,000

Yes	Button D
No	Button C

6. Here are some figures for the Btu output of one foot of N85-L Heatrim.

220°	800 Btu/hr/ft.
170°	480 Btu/hr/ft.

EXHIBIT 1

How many feet of this Heatrim at 220° would give the equivalent heat of 10 feet at 170°?

10 feet	Button C
8 feet	Button B
6 feet	Button A

7. If our house requiring 108,000 Btu/hr is fitted with a system having an average hot water temperature of 220°, it will need 135 feet of N85-L Heatrim. This is the figure you will get using the table on page 8 of your Heatrim Installation Manual. But if you estimate that the system must supply only about 81,000 Btu/hr (due to the vagrant heat sources), this means:

The system could get by with less Heatrim.	Button C
The system could get by with a lower temperature.	Button B
Both of the above are correct.	Button A

8. On the last page we mentioned that the outdoor design temperature for a house in Chicago is 10°F. Does this mean that this is as cold as it ever gets there?

Yes	Button C
No	Button B

9. Every heating man knows that water in a boiler system designed for an average temperature of 220° is not boiling because:

It is not hot enough.	Button C
It is under pressure.	Button B
Both of these reasons.	Button A

10. Which of these arguments is not applicable to the one-pipe system?

It is easy to balance.	Button D
It is cheaper.	Button C
It is easy to turn off individual pieces of radiation.	Button B

11. Is the most important aspect of the installation procedure the problem of keeping labor costs down?

Yes	Button B
No	Button A

12. Which of these would you select as the best reason for demanding the use of test-rated equipment?

It keeps the total price of the job down.	Button D
It allows for a more efficient installation procedure.	Button C
It promises safety for a closely engineered job.	Button B

EXHIBIT 1 (concluded)

office was put in charge of the experiment, and our plan of operation was carefully explained to him. It was to proceed as follows:

1. A multiple-choice examination covering the "Six Points" was to be given to each participant. Some of these questions are reproduced in Exhibit 1.
2. Directly thereafter, he or she was to be introduced to the Auto-Tutor and asked to take the short programed course.
3. Immediately following completion of the course, the same examination was to be given.
4. Ninety days later, the same examination was to be given for the third time.

Some samples of the time for completing the AutoTutor course and the number of errors made in all the examinations are shown in Exhibit 2.

Each participant was assured that he was merely assisting us with a teaching experiment and that its results would in no way affect his position with the company. The examination papers were coded, and the only identifying mark on them was that indicating "salesman" or "office employee." No one but the person giving the test and the participant himself would ever know "who got what." In each case the second and third examinations came as complete surprises, the students not having been told that they were part of the plan. We wanted to test the teaching system, not the ingenuity of the students.

Reaction ran the usual gamut from something less than enthusiasm to active interest in this new game.

OUR FINDINGS TO DATE

We experimented with 75 people and kept accurate records of the number of errors they made on each test and on the machine in addition to the amount of time it took to complete the machine portion of the course. Our sampling was small; in fact, the final test, at the time this paper is written, has been given in only one office; but a specific pattern is beginning to form.

In the main, the office personnel and the new salesmen have been the most receptive to the plan. They also have averaged higher grades than the experienced salesmen on the post-machine examinations. If this pattern continues, we may use programed instruction to train new people only—or to present new material to the more advanced employees. The review aspect of the program seems less successful.

Student reaction is interesting:

1. There appears to be a strong tendency to stay away from anything that resembles an examination. It is vital, therefore, that all participants be carefully oriented, with full explanations of

ERRORS AND COMPLETION TIMES

Code No.	Errors on Pre-Questionnaire	Errors on AutoTutor	Errors on Post-Questionnaire	Errors on Questionnaire 90 Days Later	Time on AutoTutor (Minutes)
P-1	6	9	0		34
PO-4	6	7	0		36
NY-1	7	6	3	5	35
NYO-3	8	10	1	4	35
N-1	6	9	1		35
NO-5	8	9	5		32
LI-1	11	7	1		35
LI-5	5	5	2		20
NE-1	5	6	1		26
NEO-5	5	5	2		15

AVERAGES

Philadelphia	5	6	1		35
New York	6	6	1	4	30
Newark	5	6	1		29
Long Island	6	6	1		30
New England	5	7	2		20

EXHIBIT 2

To the Assigned Instructors:

Suggested Procedure for Using the Mark II AutoTutor Teaching System

First of all, don't panic when you are asked to participate in the test program being developed with the aid of an automated teaching machine. True, it is a machine . . . but it is subject to your command! And it is designed as another aid in the scientific world of training. And don't let the word "automated" throw you either; professionals outside of our company have developed the machine and have merely adapted currently available training materials—in this instance, "The Six-Point Program for Hydronic Heating"—for simplified, yet thorough, instructional purposes.

You will personally be instructed in the operation of the AutoTutor . . . and, after that, we request your sincere participation in this test program, which can offer great opportunities if the program is handled thoroughly.

Before a participating "student" gets a chance to try the AutoTutor, please have the individual complete one of the four-page questionnaires without any reference source or outside help. These questionnaires will be provided to you when the machine is personally delivered to you by a member of the Sales Personnel Development Unit.

Then it will be necessary to explain the basic purpose of the machine, how it is properly used, and the test subject matter that will be covered by the participant "on the screen" and "by pushing the buttons."

Also, remind the student that every mistake is counted by the machine and that bluffing will only trip up the individual in subsequent frames of the film strip.

At this point it would be wise to open the top of the machine and point out (1) the counting mechanism, (2) the film strip, (3) the fact that all the student will be concerned with is the front of the AutoTutor, since you will have the top under lock and key, and (4) the 30 minutes (approximately) that will be required to complete the Six-Point Program materials being developed with the AutoTutor.

The first few frames of the film strip will clarify any haziness that the individual may have about the method of operation. After progressing for several of the opening frames, you note that the individual has complete confidence in himself with the machine, and that you may excuse yourself from him until he notifies you that he has completed the program being tested. Some initial reactions will be that it's almost like a game and doesn't seem to be too difficult; however, each frame adds an-

EXHIBIT 3

other bit to the firm foundation upon which the rest of this training technique is built.

Time the individual. This will give the Sales Personnel Development Unit additional information about the length of time required to thoroughly digest such a training program as this one is.

Next, provide the student with a duplicate copy of the questionnaire and have it completed, in your presence, as soon as possible. Then, keeping the second questionnaire as well as the first questionnaire which you retained prior to the start of the student's actual usage of the machine, thank the individual for participating in the test program.

After the student has departed from your presence, the following information should be recorded on the top of the second questionnaire:

1. Code number (explained below).
2. The actual number of minutes required to complete the course material.
3. The number of errors recorded on the counter.

Be certain to reset the counter after each individual uses the machine. This confidential number should be retained by you and marked on the student's second questionnaire. It is not our intention to show off the brightest and/or show up the slowest; the Sales Personnel Development Unit is trying out the AutoTutor technique for training our personnel by one of the newest and best methods developed, and the experience of these district field tests will aid us in evaluating the machine's future possibilities in our programing.

Incidentally, the top must be kept closed (and locked) during operation of the machine. Room lights can actuate the solenoid switch and jump the frames forward. Locking the top discourages added curiosity and provides the instructor with an accurate count of any mistakes made by the student.

The following code numbers have been assigned:

NE ....New England District
NY ....New York District
P ....Philadelphia District
N ....Newark District
LI ....Long Island Sales Office

Thus, NY-1 indicates the first sales representative to use the questionnaire in the New York District (prior to using the test program in the Auto-Tutor). NY-1A indicates the first sales representative's second questionnaire (completed immediately After using the machine). Then would follow NY-2 and NY-2A, NY-3 and NY-3A, etc., for New York District salesmen using the AutoTutor.

And don't just limit the machine usage to sales representatives. Office personnel should be encouraged to try the AutoTutor. Similarly, NYO-1 would indicate the first Office personnel to use the questionnaire in the New York District (prior to using the test program in the AutoTutor); and NYO-1A would be this individual's code number on his second questionnaire (completed immediately After using the machine.) New York District would then follow with NYO-2 and NYO-2A, NYO-3 and NYO-3A, etc.

The district person assigned to handle the machine should also maintain a list which relates the users' names to the code numbers assigned. At a later date (60-90 days) a third questionnaire is to be forwarded in bulk quantities to each participating district which will have all participants complete the third questionnaire and mail it directly to the Sales Personnel Development Unit for processing and tabulation. Students will not have to sign their names to the third questionnaire, as the assigned suffix (for example: NY-2B, P-7B, NO-6B, NYO-4B, etc.) is all that is required to tie in the Belated third questionnaire with the two completed previously by each sales or office participant.

Sales Personnel Development Unit
American-Standard Plumbing and Heating Division

EXHIBIT 3 (concluded)

what we are trying to do. (The detailed instructions issued to the instructors are reproduced in Exhibit 3.) There is measurably improved cooperation, we find, when full explanations are given.

2. The student must be permitted some degree of privacy and be given a pencil and some paper so that he can do any necessary figuring.

3. In two of the questions we asked, there was a possibility of misinterpretation. Programs therefore must be continually edited and validated.

We also discovered several advantages as well as several possible disadvantages of mechanical teaching. The advantages are as follows:

1. Technical material can be presented without expert instructors.
2. Material can be widely disseminated.
3. The trainers and the staff of the Sales Personnel Development Unit always know exactly what material is presented and how.
4. Material can be presented whenever the student "has a few moments."

The possible disadvantages are as follows:

1. The initial cost of programed material is rather high.
2. No experienced instructor is available to assist students individually.
3. Students who would like to discuss the various points with other students—as they would in a formal classroom—are frustrated because they cannot do so.

The advantages appear to outweigh the disadvantages, and our present plans call for expanding the program. We wish, however, to make haste slowly and to test the results fully before a decision is made to adopt mechanical teaching as another instructional device in our over-all training program.

Albuquerque Division
ACF Industries, Incorporated

From *A* to *Z*: Further Company Experiments in Programed Learning

By LEO W. GOEBEL

The Albuquerque Division, ACF Industries, Incorporated, is a prime contractor to the Atomic Energy Commission. It has approximately 2,000 employees. Its educational programs consist of in-hours courses on special subjects, including indoctrination, safety, security, positional tolerances, quality control, application and main-tenance of machine tape control, and other technical subjects. ACF also conducts two apprenticeship programs—machinist and elec-trical maintenance—as well as an Educational Benefits Program, chiefly for executives and engineering and technical personnel.

Three classes using TMI-Grolier programed materials were con-ducted for apprentices from January 1 to September 1, 1961. These classes included "Algebra I," with 11 students enrolled and 11 com-pletions; "Algebra II," with 11 students enrolled and 11 completions; and "Fundamentals of Electricity (DC)," with three students en-rolled and three completions.

The reasons cited by company officials for choosing self-instruction materials were:

1. To learn and utilize new methods of teaching.
2. To reduce the cost of small classes.
3. To increase the effectiveness of teaching small classes.
4. To provide for adequate self-instruction when an instructor is not available.

LEO W. GOEBEL is Apprentice Coordinator for the Albuquerque Division of ACF Industries, Incorporated.

5. To provide more effective utilization of the instructor's time.

The instructors reported that they liked the programed self-instruction idea and that they felt the TMI-Grolier materials were satisfactory. An important feature, they believe, is the continuing development of more advanced programs in mathematics. Student opinion of the programed instructional material was reported to be "good." The dread of make-up work has been removed, since each student always starts where he quit when he last attended class. In addition, if he falls behind or misses classes, he can make up the work at his own convenience without dependence on an instructor.

Albuquerque Division Training Section personnel indicated general satisfaction with the results of the programed instruction. A pre-test at the beginning and a post-test given at the end of the algebra courses showed that the classes made adequate progress. No pre-test was used for the "Fundamentals of Electricity" course, but again the instructors were satisfied with the progress made by their students. Still another indication of company satisfaction with programed self-instruction materials is the fact that it is continuing to use the algebra and electricity courses during the new instruction period which started in September 1961.

Only one deficiency in the self-instruction materials was mentioned. The administrators and instructors felt that the algebra courses did not have enough written problems. Additional problems would be helpful in providing the students with more practice in developing skills in mathematical reasoning.

Schering Corporation

By ROBERT E. FINLEY

In the fall of 1960 Schering Corporation commissioned Basic Systems Inc. to write a 783-frame program for use in a training course for detail men on a new ethical drug, according to Dr. Katharine H. Hain, Schering's Director of Medical Services. Dr. Hain, speaking before American Management Association's Special Conference and Exhibit on Programed Learning and Teaching Machines, held in Los Angeles in November 1961, described the drug—griseofulvin, which Schering manufactures and markets under the trade name Fulvicin—as well as the programed course.* Fulvicin is a drug which, although taken orally, lodges in the keratin layer of the skin and has the power to kill tineas by interfering with their growth. (Tineas are superficial fungi which are the source of ringworm and athlete's foot.) Schering decided to commission a program for training in the uses and characteristics of this drug because, at that time, it was the newest product to be developed by the firm.

Basic Systems Inc. worked with the staff of the Grace-New Haven Hospital and with physicians from the Yale University School of Medicine while programing the course. Dr. Hain pointed out that close liaison was maintained between the programers and Schering's medical and training staffs. The programed material was presented by text rather than by machine for three principal reasons: (1) Mechanical presentation has shown no advantages over textual presentation for this type of material; (2) it is cheaper; and (3) it is more convenient since it can be mailed to and carried about by the students. The program was of the constructed-response rather than the multiple-choice type because of a belief that the latter exposes the student to false information while the former does not and, at the same time, does require him to do something—give an answer—thus enhancing the learning process.

The text itself is divided into three sections whose frames run across from one page to the next, rather than from the top to the bottom of the same page. Thus the student writes his answer to the frame on the page where the question is printed and turns to the next page, where he finds the answer printed on one side and the next frame on the other. So he proceeds through the text until the end of the first section and then turns back to the beginning of section two, from which he continues through again in exactly the same manner, and so on through the third section. The obvious advantage of this textual arrangement, Dr. Hain explained, is that it

---

* See Margulies, S., and Lewis Eigen (editors), *Programed Instruction*, John Wiley & Sons, Inc., 1962, for a detailed account, by Dr. Hain, of Schering's experience.

lessens the possibility of the student's consciously or unconsciously cueing himself.

Once the programing had been completed, Schering decided to experiment with the text in the following manner. The company divided the detail men who were to be trained in Fulvicin into two groups, neither of which was informed that an experiment was being carried out. The first was a control group, and its members were instructed in the conventional manner. Each of its 19 members was informed in advance that he would be trained and tested on Fulvicin during a coming training session. Each was provided with a "backgrounder," a 25-page pamphlet containing pertinent scientific and medical information. Sample brochures and promotional material were also given to each man, all the members of the group had medical dictionaries, and some had sizable private medical libraries. A lecture, lasting four hours and 45 minutes, was delivered by a doctor on Schering's clinical research staff. Dr. Hain mentioned that no one knows as yet just how much time the men spend studying the backgrounder and other material but that Schering is attempting to find out. At the end of the lecture the group was told it would be tested two days later and was urged to review any notes made and all other relevant material.

The second group—that instructed by the programed text—consisted of 14 men, two of whom were Cuban with but fair English skills. These men received the programed text in the mail some eight to ten days in advance of the training session. None was told that he would be examined on the text, which contained precisely the same information that was covered by the lecturer to the first group. No special instruction was given other than a request to complete the program. Schering sent the program in advance for two main reasons, according to Dr. Hain: (1) To spend classroom time on it would have defeated the purpose of the experiment, and (2) Schering wanted to discover whether its detail men could find some ten hours for study on their own time in such complex subjects as mycology and dermatology. The members of this second group took a test similar but not identical to the one taken by the first group even though they were not instructed by a lecturer. The test was more difficult than usual, and it asked for more detailed knowledge of factual material than Schering normally expects of trainees. The mean grade of the control group was 60.1; that of the program-instructed group was 91.09. The reaction to programed instruction was unanimously favorable; all said they had learned more about Fulvicin than they had from other courses on other products given in the conventional manner.

Though Schering feels that no definite conclusions can be reached from just one such experiment, it has followed this course with an entire programed course on corticosteroids. It is very complex and much longer, consisting of 1,300 frames. It, too, was developed by Basic Systems Inc. in cooperation with Schering's staff and Dr. Hans Zinsser of the College of Physicians and Surgeons of Columbia University. The students' reaction to this course was the same as their feeling about the first course: They liked it, and they felt that they had learned more.

Schering's initial impression, Dr. Hain concluded, is that programed instruction may well be a technique of teaching which can effectively increase the amount of knowledge gained by its detail men, reduce classroom time for both the students and the instructors, and thus make better use of its professional training staff.

Mead Johnson Laboratories

By ROBERT E. FINLEY

Mead Johnson Laboratories, whose headquarters is in Evansville, Indiana, manufactures and markets pharmaceutical and nutritional products. Its sales representatives call on doctors, hospitals, and druggists to promote distribution of their products by influencing doctors and hospital staffs to recommend and use the company's products and druggists to carry and promote the line. The detailing work with doctors and hospitals requires an extensive knowledge of nutrition and physiology and of the company's and its competitors' products.

Three to six weeks after hiring and indoctrination by their field supervisors, the new sales representatives participate in a four-week training program at the company's headquarters. This course includes all the basic knowledge the men need as well as training and selling skills. One important area of knowledge is infant nutrition and the formula products (Enfamil, Dextri-Maltose, and so on) which the company markets. Programed learning covers infant nutrition and infant feeding. In behalf of Mead Johnson, The Industrial Education Corporation has developed four courses with more than 1,000 frames embracing some 300 facts, figures, terms, and concepts. These courses are: (1) "Infant Nutrition," (2) "Infant Feeding," (3) "The Mead Johnson Laboratories Formula Product Groups," and (4) "Specific Product Characteristics."

The courses are given as night assignments, and they are followed by lectures and practice sessions during the day. No other reading matter on the subject is assigned. The lectures and practice sessions are identical to those in force before programing. The test given following the programed courses is the same as that for past classes in which knowledge was gained through reading texts and manuals. Roger H. Zion, sales training director for Mead Johnson Laboratories, predicted in the fall of 1961 that his October class of sales trainees would boost the average on the test to 91 per cent from the 82 per cent average attained by classes before programed instruction was introduced.

Zenith Sales Corporation

By ROBERT E. FINLEY

In August 1961 Zenith Sales Corporation of Chicago introduced its line of color television sets to its own sales force and its distributors. The introduction required educating the salesmen and distributors in how color TV works and in the special features and performance characteristics of the Zenith line. A course of programed instruction was chosen to impart this necessary knowledge.

A 202-frame course covering more than 70 facts, figures, and terms was developed by The Industrial Education Corporation for this purpose. The course is divided into three sections: (1) how color TV works, (2) Zenith's superior dependability-of-performance characteristics, and (3) features and model numbers of the entire Zenith line of color TV sets. The course was initially presented as part of an introductory meeting for distributors. Although no retention tests were given, the response was so enthusiastic that distributors requested extra copies of the course for their own sales forces.

After this success, Zenith is now seriously considering the development of a shorter version for retail sales personnel.

ACCENT ON THE MACHINE

The term "machine" is used to describe even such a means of programed instruction as a text or workbook. Obviously, too, a multiplicity of devices from the tape recorder through television to complex electronic simulators are teaching machines—many of them incorporating the principles of programed instruction.

Tape-Recorded Programing for Information Service Training

By ROBERT BRINK

W e began to explore the possibilities of the programed-course type of training as the result of an article in a popular magazine about a young New York consultant who had had some quite startling successes in applying the principles of reinforcement to training programs in the Navy and, later, to a myriad of educational and industrial training situations. Our company, as a consequence, engaged his services as consultant to help us prepare an initial training course, based on reinforcement principles, for our information operators.

The popular belief is that an information operator's job is quite simple—that she is required only to look in the directory and report the telephone number if she finds it; if not, she tells the customer she doesn't have it. Actually, in the metropolitan Los Angeles area an operator is supplied with six directories containing over 2 million listings to which she may have recourse in searching for any particular number. Furthermore, she receives a daily supplement for each directory showing new and/or changed listings. Then, too, customers rarely ask for listings in precisely the same way as they are worded in the records; so there is necessarily a great body of practice which our operators must be taught with respect to search procedures, questioning techniques, and reporting. In the Los

ROBERT BRINK is Traffic Training Staff Coordinator for the General Telephone Company of California, in Santa Monica.

Angeles central directory alone there are some 3,500 listings for the name "Johnson," for instance, yet our objective is to provide a report acceptable to the customer within less than 40 seconds, on the average, from the receipt of his request. In fact, 20 to 30 per cent of the numbers are quoted by the operators within 15 seconds.

This emphasis on speed may seem excessive. However, it must be remembered that supplying information is a non-revenue-producing service. Its provision costs over $2 million annually in our California company alone. So, taking the 40-second average-disposition interval as a guide, it is apparent that any training approach which reduces this average by only one second would produce a saving of $50,000 annually. Furthermore, the grade of service acceptable to our subscribers and to the Public Utilities Commission of California will not tolerate an error factor higher than 1.7 per cent. Since an operator in a busy office will handle more than 600 calls a day, she cannot make any errors on more than ten calls if she is to achieve the accuracy we demand.

We are caught between the Scylla of providing a high grade of service and the Charybdis of doing so economically and extremely quickly. So the complexities of information service are far greater than might be apparent at first.

The Training Program Described

In our work with the consultant we spent three months in developing our initial training course. He confided to me that despite his experience in developing many types of reinforced-learning programs, ours was by all odds the most difficult on which he had collaborated because of the problems inherent in establishing criteria for individual judgment. It has been pointed out by educational psychologists that performance in the initial learning situation is of lesser practical importance than the degree of transfer that can be effected to the job situation. By "transfer" I believe they mean, principally, the ability to apply the skills that have been learned through the program to problems that are not implicit in the examples provided in the program.

The question, therefore, is: How can learning or training itself be so manipulated as to produce the maximum transfer to the job? It is generally accepted that in any specific application the transfer is improved by increasing the amount of similarity between the training situation and the job situation. In our own application we were faced with the fact that our principal requirement is for vocal exchange between an operator and a customer. After some consideration and study we felt that the use of tape-recorded instruction would more nearly approximate our job situation than a machine whose programed instruction would be primarily visual. But we had to determine first of all the nature of the terminal behavior we were striving for. (I shall later discuss how we established our goals and our measurement devices for determining the success of the training.)

On the basis of our original premise that training could best be accomplished by simulating the job-performance situation by audio-tape, we started preparing the program with the assistance of our consultant. A meeting of minds was not always easily arrived at. I must admit that much of our difficulty in reaching agreement on the sequence of material and the method by which it should be taught resulted from very firm preconceptions on the part of myself and the woman on my staff, Mrs. Hasty, who collaborated with me. A good part of our time was concentrated on weeding out those items which by analysis and careful consideration were found to be unnecessary to implanting the terminal behavior which we wanted the trainees to possess.

Even if we had decided at some point to discard programed learning completely, I feel that our expenditure would nevertheless have been worthwhile. We have been forced to take a hard look at our training goals. As a result, we have clarified differences in practice between one office and another; we have been able to simplify our reporting procedures and phraseology as they are taught to the girls; we have defined more precisely what we expect of the girls; and we have gotten down to teaching those things that are actually required on the job.

In the design of our course we have attempted to establish "task set" (inductive basis) by frequent use of such a phrase as "Suppose a customer were to make the following request?" thereby giving meaning to each problem and establishing a realistic framework within which to consider its solution. We have made liberal use of what I call "walk through" calls during which we take a student step by step through the procedures necessary to arrive at a proper report. The characteristics of these calls have been very carefully designed to help the student establish criteria by which to judge her subsequent decisions. Then we provide extensive practice calls with the complexity of the required recall quite low for each reinforcement.

We have done our best throughout to provide an optimum amount of review material with the result that there is a total of more than 600 practice examples in the course. Incidentally, we feel that if there are several ways to say the same thing, we should use them all. Redundancy in this case is a virtue.

In addition to the lesson tapes we have used other teaching aids, including instructor manuals which explain equipment operation and training-room administration; student workbooks which provide drill material and list examples for purposes of comparison; periodic written quizzes, in multiple-choice form, as a check on learning progress; and a classroom analysis form on which to record each student's progress and completion schedule.

In choosing the hardware for our course we have again attempted to simulate the actual job situation as nearly as possible in order to facilitate transfer. A student sits at a training desk which is identical, in appearance and dimensions, to the one she will occupy as an operator. She wears the headset she will have as an operator, and it plugs in no differently, but it connects her to her individual tape recorder, which is remote from her position. Control of the starting and stopping of her recorder is in the student's hands so that she is completely self-paced, as I shall explain later.

DISAPPOINTMENTS AND IMPROVEMENTS

The product of our collaboration with our consultant was a tape-recorded course which we tried out in our pilot office in Long Beach. Our initial results were vastly discouraging. In the first place, for each practice call we had had to provide on the tape an arbitrary interval of silence during which the student was to search her records and make the appropriate response or report. Since the length of time required to make a search varied widely among the students, self-pacing was impossible and led to two kinds of frustration: Fast students were frustrated because they were able to give responses considerably ahead of the reinforcement, which weakened the reinforcement through want of immediacy. Slower students were frustrated by hearing the reinforcement prior to giving their response. In order to make self-pacing possible, we have recorded an inaudible tone at the point where the girl is to start her search. This tone stops the recorder. When she has completed her response, she presses a button, and the recording gives the reinforcement. This has proved a happy solution to our self-pacing problem.

Our second cause for discouragement was the test results. In the past we had determined training success by a so-called "evaluation review," which consisted of a battery of approximately 40 fictitious calls. Disposition time was recorded for the full battery and weighted against that of an experienced operator. Errors in procedure, phraseology, and reporting were noted by the instructor, and two factors —speed and accuracy—were read into constructed tables to determine a single weighted score of performance ability. With this criterion our program-trained girls were not generally achieving passing scores. However, we found little or no correlation between student grades on the evaluation review and subsequent performance on the job as observed by the floor supervisors. So we went back to take another good look at this concept of transfer.

Were we, perhaps, attempting to train a girl to perform the job while asking her to pass an arbitrary test which was not, in itself, a valid measure of her performance ability? In our course we cover 47 varied conditions and types of calls and reports. In the progress of an average day's work, while an operator will deal with many of these situations, she will meet the simpler ones much more often. The problem seemed to be that our evaluation review, which was designed to test all the conditions which had been taught in the initial training, was not a true measure of performance ability because the frequency with which any given condition appeared on the job was not realistically represented by the review.

Our next step, therefore, was to devise a new testing procedure which we call the "personal index." Rather than evaluate fictitious calls, we sample 100 actual commercial operating calls in groups of 20 to 30 at a time over a period of four days immediately after training. By this method, too, disposition time and accuracy are recorded, and an index figure is computed for each trainee. The results of this method of measuring *actual* performance convinced us that the course was doing a better job of training than we had at first believed.

However, we were still not fully satisfied. Many simulated conditions were not being learned well enough to provide a high degree of transfer. So we began a process of detailed item analysis. We monitored a number of students individually through the full course and kept a cumulative record of all their responses. Then we analyzed our results to determine those areas where we had failed to provide enough practice with reinforcement and/or those lessons in which the explanation of the conditions to be met and the practices to be followed in meeting them were apparently unclear, thereby failing to provide the trainee with sufficient criteria on which to base her responses. On the basis of these data we completely rewrote the course, always keeping the new material within the format of the reinforced-learning concept. When tests showed the new course to be effective, I submitted the revised manuscript to our consultant in order to be sure that we had not gone off base in our techniques. When he concurred in the changes, we re-recorded the course of taped instruction, and it is now in operation in four of our offices in the Los Angeles extended area.

The results that we have achieved with the current program have been quite satisfying. In the first place, we have been able to reduce the length of our initial training, and therefore its cost, by 40 per cent. We had used ten days for information training prior to this time, and as a result of this course we have reduced the training time to six days.

This does not mean that the girls are being trained all six days by tapes; they spend the first two days in receiving taped instruction, and these lessons are interspersed with live discussions by the instructor on certain items which lend themselves better to such treatment. The discussions also relieve the otherwise pressing concentration needed during the taped lessons.

On the third day the students go to the commercial operating board. There they perform normal work, insofar as their training to that point allows, under the direct supervision of their instructor, who is plugged in with them at the board to keep them from going too far astray. Then they come back to the tapes on the fourth day for the rest of the recorded lessons.

They spend the fifth day on the commercial board again. On the sixth day of training, normally the Monday after the intervening weekend, a rather extensive series of review calls is provided by the instructor in order to determine those areas in which a student may be weak and possibly have to repeat a segment of the course. By Tuesday of the second week students are ready to go on the board as members of the workforce. From this point on they are subject to periodic progress observations from which are computed the personal indices I described earlier.

The period of probation for new employees in our company is three months, after which this decision must be made: Does this girl meet our specifications, or is she subject to release? So we evaluate terminal behavior not only at the conclusion of training, though this evaluation is of importance to us from the standpoint of how well we are training the girls. More importantly, we determine how well they have developed in speed, accuracy, and over-all ability just prior to the end of their three-month probationary period. For this purpose, too, we use the personal index for all operators, on a monthly basis, as a check on individual performance. The factors used are speed and accuracy. Operators are measured and weighted individually by the same criteria which we use to determine our over-all office service index. Our objective is 97 per cent, and we consider 90 per cent or over as acceptable.

We have trained 62 girls by means of the reinforced-learning program in Long Beach, 24 of whom have completed their three-month probation period. The average personal index achieved during their third month has been 92 per cent—which exceeds the acceptable level. Six of the 20 were above the 97 per cent top objective, and only six were below 90 per cent. Meanwhile, the quality of service in the office has greatly improved as students trained under the new method have been absorbed into the force, and the cost of providing service has declined. So we feel that the program is eminently successful.

OTHER BENEFITS FROM THE TRAINING PROGRAM

We have realized several ancillary benefits from the new course. One has been to standardize our training not only among students in one office but among offices throughout our company. This has obvious advantages, principally in subsequent on-the-job supervision and interoffice transfers.

Second—and this benefit is not necessarily intrinsic to the tape-recorded programing—we have a ready library of refresher training material which can be given as need arises to experienced operators. Such refresher training or training of rehires and girls with previous experience elsewhere can be carried on concurrently with a new training class—since all students work independently—and without requiring additional instructor time. This has provided an additional saving over and above the initial 40 per cent reduction in training cost.

Third, the instructor, being freed of much of her previous responsibility for teaching routine material, is able to give closer attention to each student's development and is also able to assume other duties while supervising the training room.

Finally, by standardizing our operator training and establishing more realistic measures of terminal behavior, I am hopeful that we shall be able to assist our personnel staff in a definitive study of applicant testing. This project is just beginning, but some of our turnover and recruitment problems may be substantially reduced as a result. Unfortunately, programing is still more an art than a science. As such it must be nurtured and developed through experimentation and practice.

System Development Corporation

A Report on the Writing and Testing of Automated Teaching Programs

By MAURICE SILBER

The System Development Corporation (SDC) began research in automated education in 1958. It was decided early in the investigatory phases of the activity that an automated teaching methodology employing a branching program that was responsive to student learning needs promised greater efficiency, in terms of learning rate and comprehension, than the various fixed-sequence programing methods. Manually conducted branching studies by SDC researchers tended to confirm this, but it was not until a refined and sophisticated branching device was employed that a significant difference in learning rate was noted.

This sophisticated device is a Bendix G-15 digital computer coupled to and controlling a large-capacity random-access slide projector. Items photographed on 35-mm slides are automatically selected and projected for the student on command of the computer through its "tutorial" computer program. After analyzing a student's response to a diagnostic question, the computer selects the next appropriate item on the basis of the programed criteria for selection of items. This procedure constitutes a simulation of the tutorial method of teaching. Of course, the method requires a large number of items in storage. With this method, however, a bright student passes over extra or remedial items, while a slower student sees as many items

MAURICE SILBER is with SDC's Center for Research in System Development.

119

as he needs to see in order to learn the material. In addition, a student's learning is constantly checked by diagnostic questions, and his difficulties with the subject matter are dealt with as they occur, before he is permitted to go on to more advanced levels of the subject.

SCOPE AND DESIGN OF THE SDC STUDIES

At first the computer was considered only a research tool; specific application was not intended. Subsequently, however, the application of a computer to actual teaching and school data-processing problems had also come under consideration.

Study of the many problems associated with the use of computers in education required the construction of a facility called CLASS (Computerized Laboratory for Automated School Systems). In the CLASS facility, the basic variables associated with programed learning and the integration of this methodology within real school environments are being studied. The application of computers to administrative data processing also will be investigated. Thus the concept of applied computer-based systems for education will be considered, using the computer as a tool for all facets of educational research.

The use of a digital computer for research in automated education provides a powerful tool for studying the areas of group interaction and individualized instruction. The computer is also useful in performance-measurement and data-reduction tasks during and after controlled experimental studies.

Since the application of the computer to actual teaching is still in a research stage, the CLASS facility will be limited at first to study and development of teaching methods. The actual teaching program will serve two purposes: (1) as material for use in studying auto-instructional variables and methods; and (2) as a basis for school environmental studies which will utilize such material to good advantage.

Initial versions of instructional programs are prepared as special texts; these texts are then used for validating the efficiency of the instructional items. After validation, the teaching program is revised for use in the computer.

2,000-ITEM INTRODUCTION TO COMPUTER PROGRAMING

SDC's Automated Education Project has developed a 2,000-item programed text to teach an introduction to computer programing. The text is now in the process of revision and will be used in a research study to test its efficacy in teaching the subject matter to computer-programer trainees.

The choice of subject matter arose from an actual teaching need within SDC. Because of its many contracts for programing large command and control systems, such as the Air Defense Command SAGE System, SDC has a training requirement for many computer programers.

The branching method of auto-instruction allows a student to learn at his own rate. For this reason some students can finish a course more quickly than others. Because of the pressing need for programers, a technique which makes it possible to utilize the services of a trainee as soon as he individually becomes technically competent affords obvious advantage over a traditional approach in which one must wait until an entire class has completed a course of instruction.

An SDC programing teacher was selected to write a branching or scrambled textbook as an introduction to computer programing. He was an expert in the specific details of the subject as well as a proficient teacher. As a first step, he was taught to program the material by the branching method.

Close and continuous liaison between the subject-matter expert and those concerned with the teaching method was required. The subject-matter expert experienced some difficulty in breaking the material into small enough units for effective automated teaching. Writing remedial items for the various branching levels was difficult, owing to the absence of actual students. In the classroom a teacher "branches" a student as a result of the student's response to a written quiz or to his verbal classroom responses. In programed instruction, however, provision of branching items must be made *in anticipation* of student difficulty since a teacher need not be present while the student is receiving the lesson. Student learning needs are best anticipated by a very experienced teacher of the subject matter.

After the program is written, it should be followed by student trials and subsequent revision. This iterative process requires careful testing of students before and after completion of the text. In this way, poorly composed items may be revised, others eliminated, and still others added where appropriate.

ACCEPTANCE TO DATE; UNSOLVED PROBLEMS

To date, these texts have been used by our computer-training organization only as supplementary instructional material. Before the texts are completed and used as an integral part of SDC's programing course, a controlled experiment will be conducted in which several classes of trainees will receive only the programed text while other sections of students will proceed through the course in the conventional manner. Both classes will be tested on the subject matter immediately upon completion of the courses as well as at a later date for retention of the material.

Students at SDC have, for the most part, enjoyed taking the course from the scrambled text. The instructors have been favorably disposed toward the book because it enables them to spend much less classroom time on introductory phases of the training program.

A problem not yet dealt with and still to be researched by the project is that of the integration of programed instruction in the total school curriculum. Even the best program cannot cope with all student learning needs. The question of how and when to deal with special individual problems as yet remains unanswered. Another problem is presented by the static, or fixed, scheduling of classes and courses in current use. As an example, a bright student can finish the SDC computer-programing course in about 5 hours—a slow student in 20 hours (these are maximum and minimum times). Extrapolation to a curriculum in which several courses are programed for automated instruction indicates that some students might finish in one-fourth the time of the slower students. How are these bright students to be dealt with? Should they be assigned additional study work, given "enrichment," or put in advanced courses? This problem will be increasingly apparent in the next few years as a greater variety of courses are programed.

It is our position that research and development in automated education must encompass, not only the variables of programing, the configuration of devices, and the integration of auto-instructional techniques, but also the structure and scheduling of the teaching and training programs for the maximal utilization of the available educational time.

Litton Industries, Inc.

Audio-Visual Techniques of Programed Instruction —A Broader View

By THOMAS P. CHEATHAM, Jr.

W e at Litton entered the field of audio-visual programed in-struction because we had a basic need for it ourselves. We were an industrial customer. Our work in the manufacture of very complex devices such as navigation and guidance equipment, to-gether with our overseas operations, had grown to such a magnitude that some of our earlier training techniques were inadequate. And the same thing was true, we realized, of our techniques for the ex-change of information overseas not just in the training and opera-tions areas but in the building and assembly of this highly complex gear. Unless we discovered new techniques and new methods, we would compromise the systems that we were placing in the hands of our U.S. naval forces and our allies.

We first looked into various techniques, studying the equipment and some of the theory. Early in 1961 we acquired the Applied Communications Systems Division of Science Research Associates because we were already a potentially large customer and, from just a straightforward business standpoint, it made a lot more sense to make what we wanted ourselves. And we definitely did have some very special needs.

THOMAS P. CHEATHAM, Jr. is Vice President of Litton Industries, Inc.

Having gone this far—in other words, satisfied our own basic production requirements—we went on to explore the opposite side of the fence. In short, we became interested in providing this type of service—equipment and programed instruction—to others. We divided the possible market into four areas: (1) the industrial, for which we already had a strong feeling; (2) the military, with which we again were rather familiar because of the nature of a large amount of Litton's business; and finally the educational area, which we divided into two segments. The first of these (3) was outside the United States; it involved transferring information to the underdeveloped parts of the world. The other (4) was of course our own national educational field.

The priority which we assigned to the four areas corresponds roughly to the order in which I have listed them. Priority in terms of the timing with which we proposed to enter these markets, that is —not necessarily in terms of need. More of that later. For the greater part of this presentation I shall concentrate on what is essentially a case history of our experience with industrial applications of audio-visual techniques of programed instruction.

MAN-HOURS AND DOLLARS LOST

Our interest—and, I think, that of industry as a whole—in the use of programed instruction and audio-visual training aids in general is to save production dollars and labor dollars. Now, the greatest loss in terms of man-hours and dollars in industry occurs on the production assembly line, primarily in the following areas:

1. Reference to—and interpretation of—blueprints, schematics, planning sheets, and the like (15 per cent).
2. Decisions on the part of the assembler; the "how to do" of the operation once the blueprint or the planning sheet has been interpreted (10 per cent).
3. Conversation with fellow workers. Women *will* talk—but assembly-line chatter costs money in wasted time, averaging as much as 10 per cent of the production hour.
4. Personal needs which we can't eliminate.

These figures have been accumulated from a variety of sources, our own operations as well as others, over the past several years. They are average figures. They are also, I believe, conservative figures; I have data which show that in a large number of typical operations the situation is much worse.

At this point, then, we still have 65 per cent of our production hour left for production. However: Rework due to errors in workmanship, such as wrong value of components, lead terminations in the wrong place, and so on takes another 20 per cent. And, last but not least, time-consuming on-the-job training or foreman instruction will account for at least an additional 5 per cent, leaving only 40 per cent for actual production assembly. To put this in terms of dollars and cents—industry, on the average, is realizing only a 40-cent return on every production dollar it spends.

It is wasting 60 cents.

The "Total" Work Station

How, you will ask, does an audio-visual system of programed instruction prevent these hours from being wasted? Here is where the so-called "total" work station comes in. A typical setup will have earphones for audio instruction and a visual diagram of the actual work which is under way. There is no more reference to, or interpretation of, paperwork of any kind. In addition to being told what to do and how to do it, step by step, the operator is shown a picture of exactly how the work should look when she has it completed. This not only eliminates any decisions on her part; it also reduces workmanship errors by at least 75 per cent and in many cases by 90 per cent. On-the-job training or instruction by the foreman is eliminated since the taped directions and the slides are all the instruction that the employee needs.

As far as eliminating conversation between fellow workers is concerned, it must be admitted that there's no possible way to keep women and girls from gossiping and chattering. There is bound to be some talking. However, owing to the fact that the worker has to perform each operation *as* and *when* instructed, we are able to eliminate almost 50 per cent of her conversation. And the fact that she wears a lightweight headset over her ears which cuts out almost all other noises helps considerably to prevent lengthy consultations on the side.

Savings Under the New System

Comparing present methods of manufacturing with the audio-visual programed-instruction system, we have found that on an average we can realize at least 84 per cent of the production hour instead of the traditional 40 per cent. This breaks down as follows:

	Per Cent	
	Old	New
Reference, interpretation	15	0
Decisions	10	0
Conversation	10	6
Rework	20	5
Instruction	5	5
Personal needs	No change	
Proportion of production hour lost	60	16
Proportion of production hour realized	40	84

As a typical example, I might cite an actual case history involving the construction of a signal amplifier. "Build" time per unit under the old method averaged about 34 hours. What happened when audio-visual techniques of programed instruction were introduced? By the end of the ninth hour, with a fairly good average achieved, the old figure of 34 hours had been reduced to 12½ hours, for a saving of 21½ hours. At the average rate for workers at this level of required skill, this represents a cost reduction of $123.61 per unit. In addition, rework due to errors in workmanship was reduced by 85 per cent.

Reports such as this add to the validity of the data previously presented. However, we realize that the productiveness of the human individual—his attentiveness, his motivation, and his interest—contributes greatly to the results. Without realizing it, we have achieved these results through the utilization of psychological principles of programed instruction.

Applicability of the New Techniques

It is easy to see that workers' readiness to accept audio-visual methods of programed instruction is highly important to industry because it is so closely related to profits in dollars and cents. It shows up directly on your profit and loss statement. The same techniques are equally applicable, of course, in the other areas—military and educational—that I have mentioned, although, as you get into the pure educational field, measures of effectiveness become a little less tangible.

Most users of programed instruction, I think, really don't care a tremendous amount about the various theories as long as they know they are doing the right thing (and understand *why* they are doing it), because this is a competitive world, and as long as they are doing it most efficiently and with the right timing. In my experience, however, there is always a great tendency to treat new things, new concepts or approaches, a little like wonder drugs; that is, we tend to use them until they start to kill about as many people as they save. In other words, the pendulum swings much too far, and then we have to bring it back. We should not lose sight of all the other media that we have available: a teaching machine is certainly not a cure-all.

There are, at the same time, many areas where the teaching machine is perhaps unique and better than anything that we've had before. This is particularly true in some of our military applications, where we have now gone the route of taking some of our very complex electronic gear—our radar, our computers, our navigation equipment, our missiles, our ships themselves—and compromising a great deal of what we can accomplish simply because of the limitations enforced by the facts of enlistment and assignment among our GI's and our sailors. We are continually hit by the requirement that we engineer equipment so that it can be operated by a GI who's finished perhaps the sixth or the eighth grade. Until we change this system—which I don't think is likely to happen in the near future—it will impose a severe constraint on the design of devices which demand a degree of sophistication many times that which you can reasonably train into a GI who doesn't particularly want to be in the Army to start with. Rather, we meet him halfway by giving him the additional aid of programed instruction—Skinnerian, Crowderian, or whatever mix may be appropriate.

We have experimented to a large extent on our assembly line. If you were to visit one of the work stations that I have described, you might see a young lady assembling circuit boards, for example. Very possibly she might never have seen a circuit board before starting work that morning, yet I would be willing to promise you that most of her circuit boards will check out as well as a trained technician's. They may not look as pretty, but they will by about the third day.

THE MACHINE'S SPECIAL ROLE

I should like to comment on statements that have been made about teaching machines replacing the teacher. I love the answer—heard via the grapevine—that a teacher who *can* be replaced by a teaching machine *should* be. But I suggest that there are some places where a teaching machine actually does better than a teacher. These are special cases, granted, but they may be important.

One problem to which I have had occasion recently to turn my attention is that of transferring educational techniques and skills from the United States to underdeveloped areas. I've had a particular interest in this because some years back I was involved in the Fulbright program which had as its objective an exchange of technical information with various countries abroad. A difficulty I ran into most markedly was the psychological barrier of national pride. In other words, it's fine that we make needed technology available; what's unfortunate is that we carry with it our own philosophy, our own culture, and our own way of looking at things. These aren't what people want, but they do want the information. The impersonal nature of the teaching machine can be extremely helpful in breaking down this barrier. The man who is not quite sure of himself and who, perhaps, is a little ashamed of his technological weaknesses in some areas would like very much to be able to feel he was on an equal par with you before exchanging views on how he might apply certain knowledge and equipment to his particular problem. Fortified by programed instruction, he may increasingly be able to do this.

The same thing might be said of a lot of our own students here in the United States who, for one reason or another, fear the teacher or fail to adjust satisfactorily to our mass instructional techniques. However, this form of sensitiveness is, I think, most pronounced overseas in areas where people have established traditions of which they are proud and which we, in a sense, can't learn without having been born and raised there ourselves. We have no right to disparage or override their way of life. What we can do is to transfer basic information to them through the impersonal and objective medium of programed instruction.

Renner, Inc.

Simulated Training Devices In Industry and Government

By C. D. LEATHERMAN

We as Americans have become almost completely conditioned to living rather complicated lives in a complex world. Our offices, homes, and cars are filled with complex devices. It's hard to realize that much of the equipment we read about or use and accept as commonplace was not even in existence 10 or 20 years ago.

Another way of underscoring our technological advances is the statement that 70 per cent of the products now being sold by General Electric were not even on the market—or, possibly, discovered —just 30 years ago. Does this statement fit your company too?

Let's consider a few specific examples. Just 30 years ago most Americans had never heard of jet airplanes, the sound barrier, split-level houses, Polaroid cameras, food freezers, guided missiles, radar, Dacron, bulldozers, V-8 engines, electric typewriters, color television, chlorophyll toothpaste, foam rubber, drive-in movie theaters, bobby soxers, toreador pants for women, Fiberglass, automatic transmission for the family car, electric razors, the United Nations, frozen vegetables, the four-minute mile, formica, bubble gum, or the atomic bomb.

These are exciting days in which we live. It continues to surprise me that we too often take such astonishing progress for granted. During this present period, progress which normally would have re-

C. D. LEATHERMAN is Executive Assistant to the President, Renner, Inc., in Philadelphia.

quired years is suddenly condensed into days or weeks or months. It took 40 years, from the Wright brothers' pioneer efforts to World War II, to push flying speeds to 500 miles per hour. But it took less than 15 years to go from 500 miles per hour to speeds of 25,000 miles per hour. I believe that one of the truly profound statements reflecting our current technological progress is the superficially rather flip remark that "if it works, it's already obsolete."

Perhaps by now we have mutually agreed that our exploding progress has created some new problems for those of us who are in management. Many responsible individuals are firmly convinced that training methodology to meet such technological advances has lagged behind. This may or may not be a fact.

I'm certain, however, that we are considering a fundamental problem in communications. Acquiring knowledge or skills is an individual matter. The basic principles of learning cannot be ignored. In order to acquire skill or knowledge, we must provide an opportunity for the trainee to practice the skill; he must be stimulated or motivated so that he wants to learn. The truth is that when the trainee is ready to learn, he learns more quickly. Furthermore, he learns more effectively if there is satisfaction during the learning process. These principles are frequently spoken of as the laws of learning: for example, the law of exercise, the law of effect, the law of readiness.

In reality, then, our basic problem is to meet the increasing demand for better-trained specialists in a shorter period of time and to maintain retention at the most efficient level. The costs involved are relative. If we can train a man to a required skill level and have him retain that skill level longer, this may be less expensive than to train him and have him lose the knowledge or skill. In the latter case we must retrain at an additional dollar cost. At some point in the training process there is an efficient training-cost index which can be fully justified and programed.

I should like to explain and summarize here a variety of simulated training devices, including some new developments, in both government and industry. I have divided my presentation into two basic parts. The first deals with training simulators using hardware; the second, with a simulated training technique using only pencil and paper.

Training Simulators Using Hardware

Perhaps the greatest strides in the simulator area have occurred as a direct result of military training requirements. The technological complexities of modern warfare involve hundreds of different skills. Many of these skills are tied directly to equipment costing millions of dollars per unit. The Boeing 707 will serve as one example. This jet aircraft contains hundreds of expensive electronic components, servo-mechanisms, and circuitry that can be serviced by only those persons who have the proper technical training.

Similarly complex equipment, such as our giant missiles and electronic systems, cannot be built in sufficient quantities to meet all of the training requirements. Recall if you will that at the Electronics Training Center of the Air Force, Keesler Air Force Base, some 20,000 electronics specialists are trained each year. And remember we also have an Army and a Navy, each with large training requirements.

Simulator for a Guided Missile System

I have chosen the Redstone missile as my example in honor of the launching vehicle which successfully orbited the first U.S. satellite on the night of January 31, 1958. The Chrsyler Corporation was asked to produce a training simulator for this missile system. It is located at the Ordnance Guided Missile School at Redstone Arsenal, Alabama. The space required for this training device is approximately the size of a large auditorium. The training simulator for the computer alone requires about one-fourth of this space.

This simulator probably cost about $1 million. The missiles themselves cost as much or even more. If we were to fire 25 of these missiles from Cape Canaveral, our cost would be at least $25 million. However, a complete checkout of all the components of the missile system can be accomplished on the training simulator, right up to the point of pushing the firing button (you can even do that and still have your training simulator). Any single portion can be similarly checked out with complete realism, time and time again. The economy involved and the effective training procedures which are possible are quite obvious.

THE 15-D-2 RADAR TARGET SIMULATOR

Now let's consider a target simulator for radar operators. This electronic device is called the 15-D-2. As is well known, the NIKE family of surface-to-air missiles is the most effective air-defense weapon of the U.S. Army. An accurate electronic guidance system assures the NIKE missiles a hit on whichever target is selected. Obviously men must be trained to a high degree of skill in order to operate this complex equipment; that is, to detect and track the small pips on the radarscope. Training missile crews with actual aircraft showing on the radarscope would not be economical. Furthermore, this type of experience would not be comparable to the conditions we would expect if the enemy used high-performance aircraft during an attack. In addition, commanders need training in the skills involved in quickly evaluating a target, deciding to engage the target with the missile, and then carrying out further steps in the air-defense mission.

The 15-D-2 Mobile Radar Target Simulator was developed by the Armed Forces Special Devices Center. This simulator can be used without impairing the effectiveness of operational functions. However, as many as six individual targets can be fed into the system, and they will appear to the operators as realistic target echoes or blips. The 15-D-2 can simulate climbing, diving, various speeds —in fact, even the launching of a missile and its movement to the point of contact with what appears to be an imaginary target.

MISCELLANEOUS DEVICES AND EQUIPMENT

Less spectacular, perhaps, is a typical training simulator for the cross-drive transmission, using the actual transmission. We have all seen many such training devices at automobile shows, fairs, and the like. Hundreds are in use in the military services and in industry.

Another type of synthetic training device is the transistor audio amplifier. Dozens of different kinds are fabricated at Keesler Air Force Base for electronics training. These devices are fully operational, light in weight, and ruggedized; the circuitry is printed photographically on a sensitized aluminum plate. Trainees are able to acquire detailed knowledge of the component by actually working with the training equipment. Similar devices include a video amplifier; a multi-vibrator; a more elaborate console for a video mapper; an AC circuit analysis trainer for resistors, inductors, and capacitors; a phase shift oscillator; a diode characterizing trainer; and a diesel electric power generating trainer. These vary from room size down to the dimensions of a medium-sized portable radio.

Burroughs Corporation has built a training device to demonstrate a step-by-step sequence for digital computers. The equipment is used to show sequentially how a computer operates and to teach programing, circuit theory, logic, computer fundamentals, and computer maintenance. The panels and circuitry may be changed by using a different plastic overlay or even tracing the circuitry with a grease pencil.

USE OF "BUILDING BLOCKS"

A similar computer training device has been built by General Electric. This was developed on the "building block" principle and can be arranged for training on specific computers as desired.

Analogous, of course, is the principle of using "building-block panels" in the step-by-step construction of an amplitude-modulated radio transmitter, fundamental and/or more advanced electronics equipment, industrial electronics components, modern communication systems, and the very large field of radar. Both the Radio Corporation of America and the Philco Corporation have manufactured various commercial packages which are readily available. The instructor begins with one basic component; next he adds another building block or component, then a third, then a fourth, and so on until a complete, functioning device has been constructed.

HUGHES AIRCRAFT VIDEOSONICS

A rather recent training innovation known as "Videosonics" may be of interest. VIDEOSONICS® is a tradename for equipment built by the Hughes Aircraft Corporation. The device is approximately the size of—and looks much like—a portable TV set. The device uses a magnetic tape which is synchronized with 35-mm color slides. Some 600 of these devices have been used to instruct employees who are engaged in the manufacture and assembly of electronic component parts. The sequence of color slides, plus the instructor's voice, tells each worker at his work bench the step-by-step procedure for his particular part of the operation. Experimental results thus far indicate improved production, decreases in errors, and large decreases in training time for new operators.

MOTION IN TRANSPARENCIES

TECHNAMATION® is a new but simple technique developed by Technical Animations, Inc., in Port Washington, New York. This makes it possible to add motion to any still transparency in any direction, at any speed, or in any combination of directions or speeds. Involved here is a basic principle of optics in which light passes through a revolving disc of transparent polarized plastic and reaches Technamated material made of birefringent translucent plastic. Continuous motion is achieved every time the polarized disc revolves. Liquids appear to flow, gases explode, gears rotate, and current flows through electrical systems. Students and instructors alike are enthusiastic about the method and about the increased student learning that results.

The list of clients is very large for this novel, inexpensive, but effective method of visual communication. Some typical users are the Chrysler Corporation, for mechanic's training; Capital Airlines, for aircraft maintenance training with reduced training times; Longines-Wittnauer, to show the working of a watch; and hundreds of others. Various evaluation studies have supported the effectiveness of this innovation as an adjunct to technical training.

A Training Simulator Without Hardware

Van Valkenburgh, Nooger and Neville, Inc., of New York, hold the basic patents on TRAINER-TESTER®, a simulated pencil-and-paper training, testing, and evaluative device. Renner, Inc., of Philadelphia, with offices from coast to coast and in Canada, is licensed to develop and produce this ingenious training device in various forms. Thus far the firm has done pioneering work in applying the technique to sophisticated training projects relating to mechanical, electro-mechanical, and electronic devices and/or systems.

Extensive work has been done in the fundamentals of electronics and in radio, where Trainer-Tester Simulators have been developed in basic electronics and for the radio transmitter, the radio teletypewriter, and the FM radio transceiver. Other simulated training devices have been produced for digital computers, vehicle maintenance, atomic weapons, re-entry vehicle test equipment, and the cross-drive transmission.

Our clients are both in industry and in the government. We have done specialized work for the Naval Training Devices Center, the Canadian Department of Defense, the U.S. Army Ordnance Guided Missile School at Redstone Arsenal, the Army Missile School at Fort Sill, the Sandia Base, the Ordnance School at Aberdeen, and the General Electric Corporation in collaboration with the U.S. Air Force.

UNIQUE BUT SIMPLE PROCEDURE

The procedure involved in the Trainer-Tester Simulator is unique but quite simple. A pencil and an eraser are all the equipment that is required. Necessary background information is given, including pictorial views, schematics, diagrams, and so forth. The trainee makes his analysis of the problem and erases his choice of an answer. Information is given him which says, "Correct. Proceed to the next step." Or, "You are not correct. Go back; re-read your problem and re-study your analysis." This is what we term "immediate feedback"; it serves as additional motivation psychologically. Chance is eliminated since the student's choice of a correct answer is made from 50 or more possibilities. He must know his subject area or the equipment in question.

We all know the importance of sequential steps in solving problems related to complicated technical equipment. With the Trainer-Tester Simulator the instructor knows immediately whether or not the trainee's thought processes were logical. At the same time he knows whether or not unnecessary steps were taken during the procedure.

Trainer-Tester Simulators provide realistic experiences in problem solving and trouble shooting without using the actual equipment, which may be very expensive and sensitive. There is no risk of damaging valuable property before the trainee is thoroughly familiar with it. In addition, let me enumerate a few other advantages: groups of trainees can progress at different rates of learning; analyzing each problem is a necessity; isolating a trouble improves markedly after practice; using these devices provides a more effective method of instruction and results in better-qualified graduates for maintenance work; equipment troubles can be simulated, whereas with the actual equipment this procedure might be prohibitive in terms of cost or might impair operational effectiveness; each trainee can be tested and evaluated individually without having to share the actual equipment with other trainees. And, from quite a different viewpoint, this simulator builds confidence in the trainee through his successes in solving problems.

THE COST FACTOR

The question of costs arises frequently and hence should be mentioned. Unquestionably, such pencil-and-paper training devices are much less expensive to develop, produce, and use than the actual equipment. Furthermore, such equipment need not be tied up just for training purposes.

Perhaps a specific example will help to illustrate the cost factor. Trainer-Tester Simulators prepared for one of the Armed Services missiles systems required 164 different exercises or problem sheets plus 45 reference sheets including schematics, wiring diagrams, and pictorial views. Twelve hundred sets, or 251,000 sheets, were produced at an approximate cost of 30 cents per sheet. This covered research, engineering, liaison, the collection of technical data, the preparation of artwork and reproducible copy, and printing.

Some of the inherent advantages may be summarized as follows: Psychologically we have motivation, feedback, and easily evaluated performance. And of even more importance in my opinion is the fact that the student is forced to use logical thinking and judgment in solving problems.

*　　*　　*

Within this brief space, we have considered a rather wide variety of training simulators using actual hardware, some operational training techniques as used in industry, a novel and effective training aid for instructors, and a simulated training and evaluative device known by the tradename of TRAINER-TESTER®. In each instance we have noted the results of evaluation studies where appropriate.

Our objective has remained unchanged—to improve the training process; in effect, to train to a higher skill or knowledge level in less time and maintain retention at the highest level practical.

All of these various training techniques involve programed learning. The applications are only as limited as our ingenuity and our imagination.

A Selected Bibliography

*Books, Brochures, Pamphlets, Articles, and
Papers on Teaching Machines, Programed
Instruction, and Related Topics*

By ROBERT E. FINLEY

Teaching machines, learning machines, programed instructional devices—call them what you will—are quite recent phenomena. The field has its pioneers, of course, pre-eminently S. L. Pressey and B. F. Skinner (some authorities even claim that Ivan Pavlov and his salivating dogs are precursors), but the physical equipment has not been manufactured in any large quantity until the past three or four years. For all their newness, however, there is an ever-growing body of literature about them, especially in the publications directed to the teaching profession. Since some enthusiasts claim that teaching machines are a threat to teachers and trainers, this last fact is not surprising, but it does explain the numerous references to articles in educational journals in the following bibliography. Few, if any, of these articles written by professional educators are of interest solely to members of the teaching profession, as their titles indicate. It is for this reason that they appear in a book designed to appeal specifically to industrial training staffs.

No attempt was made to compile an exhaustive bibliography of the field; such an attempt would most likely be futile, anyway, so quickly are the articles proliferating. Those wishing further references are directed to the section "Bibliographies" in the following pages. The main sources of this *selected* bibliography are (1) those articles, papers, and the like which have been collected by American Management Association's library staff and (2) *Teaching Machines and Programed Learning: A Bibliography,* compiled by Ina Campbell of the Teaching Materials Corporation (A Division of Grolier Incorporated). I wish to express my gratitude to Miss Campbell and to C. J. Donnelly of the same organization, both of whom have helped the editors of this present book in many ways.

Nor has there been any attempt to divide the entries according to their degree of immediate comprehensibility; their titles, once again, seem to be sufficiently indicative of the nature of their contents. But many references collected were eliminated from the original list when examination or common sense suggested that they were too abstruse or not general enough in their appeal.

Derivatives of the word "program" are spelled variously with one "m" and with two, depending upon the original editor's or author's own usage, when that was definitely known.

SPECIALIZED PERIODICALS

AID: Auto-Instructional Devices for Education and Learning, Institute of International Research and Development, Lubbock, Texas.
Audio-Visual Communication Review, National Education Association, Department of Audio-Visual Instruction, Washington, D.C.
Automated Teaching Bulletin, Rheem Califone Corporation, Los Angeles, California.
The Journal of Mathetics, Box 3232, University, Alabama.
Journal of Programed Instruction, The Center for Programed Instruction, Inc., New York City.
Programed Instruction, The Center for Programed Instruction, Inc., New York City.
Teaching Aids News Letter, Saddle Brook, New Jersey.

BOOKS, BROCHURES, AND PAMPHLETS

Carpenter, Finley, "The Teaching Machine," in *Recent Research and Development and Their Implications for Teacher Education,* American Association of Colleges for Teacher Education, Chicago, Illinois, 1960.
Corrigan, Robert E., *Automated Teaching Methods: A Solution to Our Educational Problems,* Rheem Manufacturing Company, New York, 1959.
Cram, David, *Explaining "Teaching Machines" and Programming,* Fearon Publishers, San Francisco, 1961.

Crowder, Norman A., *The Arithmetic of Computers* (a programed text), Western Design, Goleta, California, 1960.

DeBernadis, Amo, *et al.*, *Planning School for New Media,* Division of Education, Portland State College, Portland, Oregon, 1961.

Eaton, Donald K., *Teaching Machines* (Curriculum Bulletin No. 211, Vol. XVII), School of Education, University of Oregon, Eugene, Oregon, March 1961.

Eigen, Lewis D., *Sets, Relations and Functions* (a programed text), The Center for Programed Instruction, Inc., New York, 1961.

Epstein, Sam and Beryl, *The First Book of Teaching Machines,* Franklin Watts, Inc., New York, 1961.

Ferster, Charles B., and B. F. Skinner, *Schedules of Reinforcement,* Appleton-Century-Crofts, Inc., New York, 1957.

Finn, James D., and Donald G. Perrin, *Teaching Machines and Programed Learning, 1962: A Survey of the Industry,* Technological Development Project, National Education Association, Washington, D. C., 1962.

Foltz, Charles I., *The World of Teaching Machines: Programmed Learning and Self-Instruction Devices,* Electronic Teaching Laboratories, Washington, D. C., 1961.

Galanter, Eugene (editor), *Automatic Teaching: The State of the Art,* John Wiley & Sons, Inc., New York, 1959.

Guide to the Use of Programmed Instruction (Curriculum Services Series No. 4), Commonwealth of Pennsylvania, Department of Public Instruction, Harrisburg, Pennsylvania, 1961.

Joint Committee Statement on the Use of Self-Instructional Materials and Devices, National Education Association, Department of Audio-Visual Instruction, Washington, D. C., 1961.

Keller, Fred S., *Learning: Reinforcement Theory,* Random House, New York, 1954.

———, and William N. Schoenfeld, *Principles of Psychology,* Appleton-Century-Crofts, Inc., New York, 1950.

Leavitt, Jerome E., and Rilla J. Edgar, *Programed Learning and Teaching Machines,* Instructional Services Section, State Department of Education, Salem, Oregon, 1961.

Lumsdaine, A. A., and Robert Glaser (editors), *Teaching Machines and Programmed Learning: A Source Book,* National Education Association, Department of Audio-Visual Instruction, Washington, D. C., 1960.

Lysaught, Jerome P. (editor), *Programmed Learning: Evolving Principles and Industrial Applications,* The Foundation for Research on Human Behavior, Ann Arbor, Michigan, 1961.

Mager, Robert F., *Preparing Objectives for Programmed Instruction,* Fearon Publishers, San Francisco, 1961.

Margulies, S., and Lewis D. Eigen (editors), *Programed Instruction,* John Wiley & Sons, Inc., New York, 1962.

Markle, Susan M., Lewis D. Eigen, and P. Kenneth Komoski, *A Programed Primer on Programing,* The Center for Programed Instruction, Inc., New York, 1961.

Mills, Annice L. (editor), *Programmed Learning and the Educational Process* (A Summary of a Conference held by The Thomas Alva Edison Foundation and Grolier Incorporated), The Thomas Alva Edison Foundation, New York, 1961.

Milton, Ohmer, and Leonard J. West, *Programed Instruction—What It Is and How It Works,* Harcourt, Brace and World, Inc., New York, 1961.

MIN/MAX Teaching Machine, Teaching Materials Corporation (A Division of Grolier Incorporated), New York.

Nesbit, Paul W., "Additional Opportunities with Automated Learning," *Nesbit's Learning Methods,* January 1961.

New Teaching Aids for the American Classroom—A Symposium, The Institute for Communication Research, Stanford University, Stanford, California.

"Not from Teaching but from Questioning," *Carnegie Corporation of New York Quarterly,* October 1961.

Programmed Instruction, McGraw-Hill Book Co., Inc., New York.

Programmed Teaching, General Programmed Teaching Corporation, Albuquerque, New Mexico.

Rigney, Joseph W., and Edward B. Fry, *Current Teaching Machines and Programming Techniques* (*AV Communication Review Supplement 3,* May-June 1961), National Education Association, Department of Audio-Visual Instruction, Washington, D. C.

Skinner, B. F., *Cumulative Record* (enlarged edition), Appleton-Century-Crofts, Inc., New York, 1961.

———, *Science of Human Behavior,* The Macmillan Company, 1953.

———, *Verbal Behavior,* Appleton-Century-Crofts, Inc., New York, 1957.

———, and James G. Holland, *Analysis of Behavior* (a programed text), McGraw-Hill Book Co., Inc., New York, 1961.

Stolurow, Laurence M., *Teaching by Machine* (OE-34010 Cooperative Research Monograph No. 6), U. S. Government Printing Office, Washington, D. C., 1961.

"Teaching Machines and Programmed Learning," *Professional Growth for Administrators, Professional Growth for Principals,* and *Professional*

Growth for Teachers, all Vol. 7, No. 5, Croft Educational Services, New London, Connecticut, December 1961.

Training Research Abstracts, Vol. I, No. 1, American Society of Training Directors, Madison, Wisconsin, January 1961.

Tutor Text, a Sample Sequence, Western Design, Santa Barbara, California.

The Western Design Tutor, Western Design, Santa Barbara, California.

What Is a Teaching Machine? Teaching Materials Corporation (A Division of Grolier Incorporated), New York.

ARTICLES: INDUSTRY, EDUCATION, MILITARY, AND GENERAL

Abma, John S., "Programming for Teaching Machines," *Battelle Technical Review,* February 1961.

"Audio-Visual Aid Speeds Output," *The Iron Age,* August 24, 1961.

"Automated 'Teacher' Revolutionizes Training," SUPERVISORY MANAGEMENT, March 1961, and THE MANAGER'S LETTER, January 20, 1961.

"Automated Teaching System Under Computer Control," *Computers and Automation,* May 1961.

"Automatic Teaching Machines: Programs Start to Appear," *Control Engineering,* October 1961.

"Automation in the Class Room," *Financial World,* December 21, 1960.

Babcock, Chester D., "The Teacher, TV, and Teaching Machines," *NEA Journal,* May 1960.

Bard, Bernard, "The Teaching Machine," *New York Post,* January 1, 1961.

Bardwell, John D., "Programed Instruction and Teaching Machines," *New Hampshire Educator,* November-December 1961.

Barlow, J. A., "Project Tutor," *Psychological Reports* (6), 1960.

———, "Teaching Machines and Educational Philosophy," *School and Society,* April 22, 1961.

Beggs, David W., "Teaching Machines and Programed Learning," *Illinois Education,* December 1961.

Bendick, Marc, "Equipment for Automated Teaching," *Datamation,* April 1961.

Bergstein, Harold, "The Computer-Based Classroom," *Datamation,* April 1961.

Beringause, A. F., "Teacher and the Machine," *High Points,* June 1961.

———, "Teaching Machine," *High Points,* May 1961.

Bissmeyer, Ollie, Jr., "Teaching Machines," *Kentucky School Journal,* November 1961.

Blyth, John W., "Teaching Machines and Human Beings," *The Educational Record*, April 1960.

Boehm, George A. W., "Can People Be Taught Like Pigeons?" *Fortune*, October 1960.

Boroff, D., "The Three R's and Pushbuttons," *The New York Times Magazine*, September 25, 1960.

Boutwell, W. D., "What's Happening in Education?" *National Parent Teacher*, June 1960.

Braley, Ian, "Will Robots Teach Your Child?" *Today's Living*, September 4, 1960.

Bruce, W. C., "Teaching Machines," *American School Board Journal*, June 1961.

Budd, William C., and Charles H. Harwood, "The Perspective of Teaching Machines," *Washington Education*, November 1961.

Bundy, McGeorge, "Science as a Way of Life," *Harvard Today*, Autumn 1961.

Bushnell, D. D., and J. F. Cogswell, "Computer-Based Laboratory for Automation in School Systems," *Audio-Visual Communication Review*, July 1961.

Bylinsky, Gene, "Robot Teachers," *The Wall Street Journal*, August 8, 1960.

Carpenter, Finley, "How Will Automatic Teaching Affect Education?" *University of Michigan Education Bulletin*, October 1959.

Cass, James, "New Tools for Teaching," *The Saturday Review*, February 18, 1961.

———, "New Tools for Teaching," *Washington Education*, November 1961.

"Center for Programed Instruction," *Audiovisual Instruction*, April 1961.

Cobleigh, I. U., "Robot Teachers and Electronic Classrooms," *Commercial and Financial Chronicle*, April 13, 1961.

Cocking, Walter D., "As I See It—Teaching Machines," *Overview*, August 1961.

"The Coming Boom in Teaching Machines," *Control Engineering*, June 1960.

"Committee Sets Initial Criteria for Programed Materials," *Programed Instruction*, May 1961.

"Computer-Based Teaching Machine Subject of Government Grant," *Computers and Automation*, April 1961.

"Computer Controls Teaching Machine," *Electronics*, January 6, 1961.

Conner, Forrest E., "What Should an Administrator's Attitude Be?" *NEA Journal*, November 1961.

Cook, Donald A., "Programmed Learning: A Revolution in Instruction," *Graduate Faculties Newsletter*, Columbia University, November 1960.

Cook, Desmond L., "Teaching Machine Terms: A Glossary," *Audiovisual Instruction*, April 1961.

Cook, F. S., "Some Advantages and Limitations of Self-Instructional Devices," *Balance Sheet*, December 1960.

Cooley, E. F., "Automated Teaching," *Computers and Automation*, July 1961.

Corrigan, Robert E., "A Solution to Some Pressing Problems in Education," *California Teachers Association Journal*, September 1960.

———, "Teaching Machines and Automated Instructional Methods," *Journal of the American Society of Training Directors*, April 1960.

Coulson, John E., and Harry F. Silberman, "Automated Teaching and Individual Differences," *Audio-Visual Communication Review*, January-February 1961.

———, "Teaching Machines Simulated by Computer," *Computers and Automation*, October 1960.

Crowder, Norman A., "Teaching Machines Are a Threat to Teachers," *School Management*, December 1960.

———, "The 'Tutor,'" *Journal of the American Society of Training Directors*, May 1960.

"Current Research," *School Libraries*, March 1961.

Currivan, G., "The New Teacher: All Electronics," *The New York Times*, June 30, 1960.

Dale, Edgar, "Self-Instruction Through Programmed Materials," *The News Letter*, Bureau of Education Research, Ohio State University, Columbus, Ohio, February 1961.

deKieffer, R. E., "Teaching Machines, Self-Instruction Devices," *Colorado School Journal*, May 1961.

Dolmatch, Theodore B., "Programed Instruction—The Managerial Perspective," PERSONNEL, January-February 1962.

Dunn, S. K., "The Progress Plotter as a Reinforcement Device," *The Journal of Mathetics*, Vol. I, No. 1, 1962.

Dunne, M. J., "Industrial Robot Learns New Jobs with Ease," *Control Engineering*, May 1961.

Edgerton, Alice K., "Machine Spelling—and How It Works," *Grade Teacher*, September 1961.

"Education," *Business Week*, September 17, 1960.

"Education," *Time*, March 24, 1961.

"Education—Push-button Proofs," *Newsweek*, September 11, 1961.

"Educators Turn to Machines and a New Method," *International Management,* July 1961.

Eigen, Lewis D., "The Construction of Frames of an Automated Teaching Program," a paper available from The Center for Programed Instruction, Inc., New York City.

———, "Some Problems in Field Testing Programs for Teaching Machines," *Journal of Educational Sociology,* April 1961.

———, "Technology and Educational Practice," a paper available from The Center for Programed Instruction, Inc., New York City.

———, and P. Kenneth Komoski, "Research Summary Number 1," a paper available from The Center for Programed Instruction, Inc., New York City.

———, "Teaching Machines Can Aid the Schools to Make Better Use of Teacher Time," *California Journal of Secondary Education,* April 1960.

"Electronic Teaching Machines—Blessing or Curse?" *Popular Electronics,* November 1960.

"Electronic Tutor and Interviewer Guided by a Computer," *Computers and Automation,* February 1961.

"Encyclopedia House Enriches Its Pitch," *Business Week,* January 21, 1961.

England, Don, and Don Estavan, "Programming a Computer to Teach," *Datamation,* April 1961.

Exton, Elaine, "Teaching Machines: Fad or Here to Stay?" *School Board Journal,* September 1960.

Feldhusen, John F., "Problems Schools Will Face in Planning to Use Teaching Machines," *Education Administration and Supervision,* 1961.

———, "Will Teaching Machines Produce Machine Teaching?" *Wisconsin Journal of Education,* 93, 1961.

Ferrer, Terry, "Can Machines Really Teach?" *New York Herald Tribune,* December 18, 1960.

Ferster, Charles B., "Studies in the Control of Eating," *The Journal of Mathetics,* Vol. I, No. 1, 1962.

Finn, James D., "Automation and Education," *Audio-Visual Communication Review,* Winter 1957, Spring 1958, and Winter 1960.

———, "Educational Technology—A New Force," *ALA Bulletin,* February 1961.

———, "The Principal Faces the New Technology," *The National Elementary Principal,* January 1961.

———, "Teacher Understanding—Keys to the New Technology," *California Teachers Association Journal,* September 1960.

———, "Teaching Machines: Auto-Instructional Devices for the Teacher," *NEA Journal,* November 1960.

Fleck, Henrietta, "More About Teaching Machines," *Forecasts for Home Economists,* October 1961.

"For Brighter Students? Teaching Machines," *Newsweek,* August 17, 1959.

Fountain, Ben E., Jr., "New Teaching Media for a New Day," *North Carolina Education,* October 1961.

Freeman, J. T., "The Effects of Reinforced Practice on Conventional Multiple-Choice Tests," *Automated Teaching Bulletin,* September 1959.

Fry, Edward, "California Steps Out with Teaching Machines," *California Teachers Association Journal,* September 1960.

———, "The Mechanical Teacher," *The Texas Outlook,* June 1960.

———, "Programming Trends," *Audiovisual Instruction,* April 1961.

———, "Teaching Machines and Reading Instruction," *The Reading Teacher,* September 1961.

———, "Teaching Machines: An Investigation of Constructed *versus* Multiple-Choice Methods of Response," *Automated Teaching Bulletin,* December 1959.

———, "Teaching Machines: The Coming Automation," *The Phi Beta Kappan,* October 1959.

Fuller, J. G., "Trade Winds: Min/Max Machines," *The Saturday Review,* March 11, 1961.

Fulton, Robert E., "The Teaching Machine," *Mechanical Engineering,* September 1961.

Fusco, Gene C., "Programmed Self-Instruction: Possibilities and Limitations," *The High School Journal,* 44, 1960.

———, "The Teacher and the Teaching Machine," *The Tennessee Teacher,* December 1960.

———, "Technology in the Classroom: Challenge to the School Administrator," *School Life,* May 1960.

Galanter, Eugene, "The Mechanization of Learning," *NEA Journal,* November 1961.

———, "The Mechanization of Teaching," *The Bulletin,* April 1960.

———, "Two Models of a Student," *Teachers College Record,* December 1960.

Gates, A. L., "Teaching Machines in Perspective," *Elementary School Journal,* October 1961.

Gilbert, Thomas F., "Mathetics: The Technology of Education," *The Journal of Mathetics,* Vol. I, No. 1, 1962, *et seq.*

Gilmore, Ken, "Teaching Machines—Blessing or Curse?" *Popular Electronics,* November 1960.

Ginther, J., "Man, Values and the Machine," *Elementary School Journal,* 60, 1960.

———, "More on Teaching Machines," *Elementary School Journal*, February, 1961.

Girson, Rochelle, "Latest on Teaching Tools," *The Saturday Review*, February 16, 1957.

Glaser, Robert, "Christmas Past, Present, and Future: A Review and Preview," *Contemporary Psychology*, January 1960.

———, and Margaret Fullick, "Programmed Learning and Classroom Instruction," *Pennsylvania School Journal*, May 1961.

———, and Halmuth H. Schaefer, "Programmed Teaching," *The Journal of Teacher Education*, March 1961.

Gorman, Alfred, "The Turn of Attention to Teaching Machines," *New Jersey Education Association Journal*, September 1961.

Gorow, Frank F., "I Wrote a Scrambled Book," *Audiovisual Instruction*, April 1961.

Grieder, C., "Place and Value of Teaching Machines," *Nation's Schools*, May 1961.

Groesberg, S. W., "The Teaching Machine . . . Pros and Cons," *Mechanical Engineering*, April 1961.

Gunther, Max, "Automation in the Classroom," *American Legion Magazine*, July 1961.

Hansen, Arnold R., "Continuity Vehicle . . . A New Approach," *Grade Teacher*, October 1961.

Heimer, R. T., "Some Implications of Programmed Instruction for Teaching of Mathematics," *The Mathematics Teacher*, May 1961.

Henderson, Robert, "Listen Son," *The New Yorker*, December 5, 1959.

Henry, William G., Jr., "What Makes a Teaching Machine Teach?" *Audiovisual Instruction*, April 1961.

"Here Is a Deluxe Version of a Computer-Type Teaching Machine," *Mid-Hudson Channel*, 10, No. 2, 1961.

Hilgard, Ernest R., "What Support from the Psychology of Learning?" *NEA Journal*, November 1961.

Holland, James G., "Evaluating Teaching Machines and Programs," *Teachers College Record*, October 1961.

———, "Teaching Machines: An Application of Principles from the Laboratory," *Journal of Experimental Analysis of Behavior*, October 1960.

———, (Review of) *Teaching Machines and Programed Learning: A Source Book*, *Contemporary Psychology*, September 1961.

Hoth, William E., "From Skinner to Crowder to Chance: A Primer on Teaching Machines," *The English Journal*, September 1961.

"How Far Are We Going with Machine Teaching?" *Personnel Journal*, December 1960.

"How Machines Do Teaching Job," *Business Week*, September 17, 1960.

"How to Buy Programmed Instruction—A Guide for Management," Basic Systems Inc., New York, August 1961.

Huffman, H., "Putting the Teaching Machine on Paper," *Business Education World,* April 1961.

———, and S. Margulies, "Teaching Machine Program for a Topic in Business Mathematics," *Business Education World,* May 1961.

Hughes, J. L., "The Effectiveness of Programed Instruction," paper available from The Center for Programed Instruction, Inc., New York City.

———, "Industrial Applications of Teaching Machines," *Journal of the American Society of Training Directors,* July 1961.

———, and W. J. McNamara, "A Comparative Study of Programed and Conventional Instruction in Industry," *Journal of Applied Psychology,* August 1961.

———, "The Potential of Programmed Instruction," PERSONNEL, November-December 1961.

Hyer, Anna L., and Robert C. Snider, "The Profession and the Machine," *California Teachers Association Journal,* September 1960.

Ikenberry, N. B., "Teaching Machines," *Elementary English,* October 1961.

"The Industrial Use of Teaching Machines," *Journal of the American Society of Training Directors,* August 1961.

"It Doubled Output in Cedar Rapids," *Factory,* September 1960.

Jacobson, John, Jr., "Teaching High School Students a College Level Course by Means of a Learning Machine Program," *Mid-Hudson Channel,* 10, No. 2, 1961.

Jan-Tausch, James, "The Big Difference That Goes into Machine Programs," *NEA Journal,* September 1961.

Keislar, E. R., "Potential of Auto-Instruction," *American Vocational Journal,* February 1961.

———, and J. D. McNeil, "Teaching Scientific Theory to First Grade Pupils by Auto-Instructional Device," *Harvard Educational Review,* Winter 1961.

Kennedy, Ward, "Electrifying the Three R's," *Pageant,* February 1961.

Klass, Philip J., "Video-Sonics Cuts Production Defects," *Aviation Week,* January 4, 1960.

Klaus, David J., "The Art of Auto-Instructional Programming," *AV Communication Review,* March-April 1961.

———, "Programming: A Re-emphasis on the Tutorial Approach," *Audiovisual Instruction,* April 1961.

Klausmeier, Herbert J., and Philip Lambert, "Teaching Machines and the Learning Process," *Educational Leadership,* February 1961.

Komoski, P. Kenneth, "Call It 'Programed Instruction'—Not a Teaching Machine," *Mid-Hudson Channel,* 10, No. 2, 1961.

———, "The Collegiate School Conference," *Audiovisual Instruction,* April 1961.

———, "Current Development and Experimentation in the Field of Programed Instruction," paper available from The Center for Programed Instruction, Inc., New York City.

———, "Programed Instruction and Its Place in Education," *Educational Conference,* 1960; also available as a paper from The Center for Programed Instruction, Inc., New York City.

———, "Programing by Teachers for the School Curriculum," paper available from The Center for Programed Instruction, Inc., New York City.

———, "Programmed Materials," *The Nation's Schools,* February 1961.

———, "Teaching Machines," *Instructor,* March 1961.

———, "Teaching Machines and Programed Reading Instruction," paper available from The Center for Programed Instruction, Inc., New York City.

———, "What Are the Schools Doing?" *NEA Journal,* November 1961.

Kowitz, G. T., "Administrating the Automated School," *American School Board Journal,* February 1961.

Kreig, Margaret B., "What About Teaching Machines?" *Parents Magazine,* February 1961.

Kropp, R. P., and H. A. Curtis, "Teaching with Machines," *Florida Education,* October 1960.

Kvaraceus, William C., "Future Classroom—An Educational Automat?" *Educational Leadership,* February 1961.

Lange, Phil, "Guide Lines for Appraising the Promise of Teaching Machines," *Mid-Hudson Channel,* 10, No. 2, 1961.

Larkin, J. W., Jr., "Explanation, Evaluation of Programmed Instruction," *Publishers' Weekly,* May 22, 1961.

Larrick, Nancy, "Teaching Machines—A Progress Report," *Library Journal,* April 15, 1961.

"Learning About Learning," *SRI-Research for Industry,* July-August 1961.

Leighton, Frances Spatz, "Remote Control Learning," *The American Weekly,* February 19, 1961.

Levine, Stanley L., and Leonard C. Silvern, "The Evolution and Revolution of the Teaching Machine," Parts 1 and 2, *Journal of the American Society of Training Directors,* December 1960 and January 1961.

Loehwing, David A., "Aids to Education: Teaching Devices Proving Their Usefulness in U. S. Schools," *Barron's,* May 16, 1960.

———, "Teaching Machines," *Barron's,* October 30, 1961.

Luce, Guy Gaer, "Can Machines Replace Teachers?" *Saturday Evening Post,* September 24, 1960, and *Reader's Digest,* December 1960.

Lumsdaine, Arthur A., "Teaching Machines and Auto-Instructional Programs," *Educational Leadership,* February 1961.

———, "Teaching Machines and Self-Instructional Materials," *The Education Digest,* December 1959.

Lysaught, Jerome P., "Industrial Training Through Programmed Learning," *Personnel Journal,* September 1961.

———, "Programmed Learning and Teaching Machines in Industrial Training," Parts 1 and 2, *Journal of the American Society of Training Directors,* February and June 1961.

———, "Programmed Learning and the Classroom Teacher," *New York State Education,* February 1961.

"Machine 'from Birds' Is Causing Revolution," *Film World,* November 1961.

"Machine Taught Electronics," *Electronics Illustrated,* April 1961.

"Machine Tutors Man for Jobs," *Business Week,* October 22, 1960.

"Machines for Teaching," *Science,* June 17, 1961.

"Machines That Teach," *Business Week,* August 26, 1961.

MacLeod, D., "Teaching Machines in Biblical Hebrew," *Christian Century,* August 23, 1961.

"Management—Robot-Run Training Programs," *Business Week,* August 26, 1961.

Margulies, S., "The Industrial Use of Teaching Machines," *Journal of the American Society of Training Directors,* August 1961.

Markle, Susan Meyer, "Inside the Teaching Machine," *The Saturday Review,* November 18, 1961.

McDonnell, G. J., "Automated Teaching," *Growth Stock Review,* July 1960.

McLellan, James, "Automated Education: A Philosophical Approach," paper available from The Center for Programed Instruction, Inc., New York City.

McNeil, J. D., and E. R. Keislar, "Individual Differences and Effectiveness of Auto-Instruction at the Primary Grade Level," *California Journal of Educational Research,* September 1961.

Melby, E. O., "TV, Teaching Machines and Teachers," *Challenge,* April 1961.

Merrill, Harwood F., "Breakthrough Ahead in Training," MANAGEMENT NEWS, September 1960.

Miller, Murray Lincoln, "Individualized Instruction," *Illinois Education,* December 1961.

Morrill, C. S., "Teaching Machines: A Review," *Psychological Bulletin,* September 1961.

Murdock, Arthur C., "Let's Try a Learning Machine," *Science Teacher,* April 1961.

Nanas, Ed, "There's a Teaching Machine in Your Future," *Electronics Illustrated,* April 1961.

Newman, Fred M., "Teaching Machines: A Primer," *Educational Screen and Audiovisual Guide,* January 1961.

Noall, M. S., "Automated Teaching of Reading Skills in High School," *Journal of Education,* February 1961.

Nordberg, R. B., "What Teaching Machines Can and Cannot Do," *Catholic Educational Review,* September 1961.

Ohles, J. F., "Approach to Machine Teaching," *School and Society,* November 19, 1960.

Olds, Robert, "Automated Machines," *Ohio Schools,* April 1960.

"On the Program: New Training Savings," *Chemical Week,* September 9, 1961.

Packer, R. E., "Education Machines—A Trend Toward Automated Teaching," *Industrial Research,* February-March 1961.

Pask, Gordon, "Machines That Teach," *New Scientist,* May 11, 1961.

Pennington, Dempsey F., Jr., "Systematic Design of Simulators: A Sales-Clerk Training Kit," *The Journal of Mathetics,* Vol. I, No. 1, 1962.

Popp, Helen M., and Douglas Porter, "Programming Verbal Skills for Primary Grades," *Audio-Visual and Communications Review,* August-September 1960.

"Practical Examinations for the Technician and Mechanic," *Journal of British Institution of Radio Engineers,* March 1959.

Pressey, S. L.,[*] "Development and Appraisal of Devices Providing Immediate Automatic Scoring of Objective Tests and Concomitant Self-Instruction," *Journal of Psychology,* April 1950.

———, "A Machine for Automatic Teaching of Drill Material," *School and Society,* May 7, 1927.

———, "A Simple Apparatus Which Gives Tests and Scores—and Teaches," *School and Society,* March 20, 1926.

[*] All four of these classic pioneering articles by S. L. Pressey are reprinted in *Teaching Machines and Programmed Learning: A Source Book,* edited by A. A. Lumsdaine and Robert Glaser.

————, "A Third and Fourth Contribution Toward the Coming 'Industrial Revolution' in Education," *School and Society*, November 19, 1932.

Price, George R., "The Teaching Machine," *Think*, March 1959.

"Programmed Learning and the Use of Teaching Machines," *Computers and Automation*, October 1961.

"Programmed Learning: Can Machines Replace Teachers?" *Time*, March 24, 1961.

"Programmed Learning: The Coming Revolution in Job Training," *Industrial Relations News*, June 1961.

"Programmed Teaching," *Financial Analysts Journal*, November-December 1961.

"Push Button Brains," *Newsweek*, October 26, 1959.

"R&D Approach Right for Education," *Chemical and Engineering News*, May 15, 1961.

Rath, Gustave J., "A New Task for the Technical Writer—Programming Teaching Machines," *IRE Transactions Engineering Writing and Speech*, January 1961.

————, and M. Weiss, "The Economic and Social Implications of Programed Learning and Teaching Machines," unpublished paper presented before the American Management Association's Conference on Programed Learning and Teaching Machines, New York, August 1961.

Reed, J. E., "Aid for the Teacher of English," *English Journal*, February 1961.

Reed, R. C., "Machines for Your Future?" *Educational Screen*, December 1959.

Rees, Louise F., "Public Librarians Must Face the Challenge," *ALA Bulletin*, February 1961.

"Reinforced Learning Course for Proof Machine Operators," *Auditgram*, April 1961.

"Robot Instructors Win Friends and Speed Assembly," *Factory*, November 1960.

"Robot-Run Training Programs," *Business Week*, August 26, 1961.

Rothkopf, Ernst Z., "A Do-It-Yourself Kit for Programmed Instruction," *Teachers College Record*, 62, No. 3, 1960.

Rothman, Philip, "Pushbutton Pedagogy," *Antioch Notes*, November 1960.

Ruark, Henry C., Jr., "Auto-Instructional Devices Alias Teaching Machines," *Oregon Education*, December 1960.

Rufswold, Margaret I., "Library Education and the Newer Media," *ALA Bulletin*, February 1961.

Rushton, E. W., "Greatly Accelerated Learning of Algebra Through Use of Programmed Materials," *The Nation's Schools,* February 1961.

"A Schoolman's Guide to Teaching Machines," *School Management,* October 1961.

Schure, Alexander, "A Case for Automatic Teaching Equipment," *Technical Education News,* May 1959.

Seligman, Daniel, "Professor Skinner's Teaching Machine," *Fortune,* October 1958.

Shafer, Susanne M., "Teaching Machines and the Social Studies," *Social Education,* February 1961.

Shaffer, Helen B., "Teaching by Machine," *Editorial Research Reports,* January 25, 1961.

Shettel, H. H., and A. A. Lumsdaine, "Principles of Programming as Applied to the Development of Two Self-Instructional Programs for Sage Operators," AFCCDD-TN-61-27/AIR-C11-61-SR-247, American Institute for Research, Pittsburgh, Pennsylvania, February 1961.

Silberman, H. F., "Teaching Machines," *Junior College Journal,* February 1961.

———, *et al.,* "Fixed Sequence *vs.* Branching Autoinstructional Methods," *Journal of Educational Psychology,* June 1961.

Silverman, R. E., "Some Features of Auto-Instructional Devices," *Journal of Higher Education,* March 1961.

Silvern, Leonard C., "An Analysis of the Teaching Machine Field and Implications for Home Study Courses," *The Home Study Review,* Winter 1961.

———, "Change in the Training Director's Job," *Journal of the American Society of Training Directors,* February 1961.

———, "Implications of the Teaching Machine for Firemanship Training," *Fire Engineering,* March 1961.

———, "The Influence of Teaching Machine Technology on Electronic Systems Maintenance Training," *IRE Transactions on Human Factors in Engineering,* September 1961.

———, "Now the Teaching Machine," *United States Review,* November 26, 1960.

———, "Principles and Techniques for Training Programmers," a paper presented to the 16th National Conference of the Association for Computing Machinery, Los Angeles; (unpublished document 5.6.15, Hughes Aircraft Company, Culver City, California, April 1, 1961).

———, "Specifications for a Component-Type General Purpose Teaching Machine of Optimum Capability for Curriculum Development-1961" (unpublished document 5.6.27, Hughes Aircraft Company, Culver City, California, June 1961).

————, "The State of the Art—Teaching Machine Technology," unpublished paper presented to the American Management Association's Special Conference on Programed Learning and Teaching Machines, New York, August 1961.

————, "The Teaching Machine for Employee Development," *Personnel Journal*, March 1961.

————, "Uniformity in Teaching Machine Technology," *AID*, May 1961.

Sindler, A. J., "Self-Instructional Analog Computer Training," *Journal of the American Society of Training Directors*, November 1961.

Skinner, B. F., "The Science of Learning and the Art of Teaching," *Harvard Educational Review*, Vol. 24, No. 2, 1954.

————, "Teaching Machines," *Science*, October 1958.

————, "Teaching Machines," *Scientific American*, November 1961.

————, "Teaching Machines," *Studies in Personnel and Industrial Psychology* (edited by Edwin A. Fleishman), Dorsey Press, Homewood, Illinois, 1961.

————, "The Theory Behind Teaching Machines," *Journal of the American Society of Training Directors*, July 1961.

————, "Why We Need Teaching Machines," *Cumulative Record*, Appleton-Century-Crofts, Inc., New York, 1961.

Slack, Charles W., "Lessons That Teach: The Theory and Significance of the Educational Revolution to Industry," unpublished paper presented to the American Management Association's Conference on Programed Learning and Teaching Machines, New York, August 1961.

————, "The Automatic Interview Machine," *The Journal of Mathetics*, Vol. I, No. 1, 1962.

Smith, Donald E. P., "Teaching Machine," *Michigan Education Journal*, March 1960.

Snider, Robert C., "Teaching Machines," *The Nation's Schools*, February 1961, and *North Dakota Teacher*, April 1961.

Stein, Jay W., "Machines That Teach Better Than Books?" *College and Research Libraries*, May 1961.

Stevens, Kimble, "Square Like Crazy in 4 Minutes," *Pageant*, May 1961.

Stevens, Traxel, "The Look of Things to Come," *The Texas Outlook*, June 1961.

Stolurow, Lawrence M., "Problems in Evaluating Automated Instruction," *Teachers College Record*, October 1961.

————, "Teaching Machines and Special Education," *Education Digest*, December 1960.

——, and Leonard J. West, "Teaching Machines and Self-Instructional Programming," *The Delta Pi Epsilon Journal*, 3, No. 3, 1961.

Stone, Walter C., "The Crisis in Education—A Mandate for Librarians," *ALA Bulletin*, February 1961.

Sturwold, Virginia G., "Sources of Self-Instructional Devices," *Audiovisual Instruction*, April 1961.

"The Teacher in the Automatic Box," *Overview*, June 1961.

"The Teacher in the Mechanical Box," *Investor's Reader*, September 27, 1961.

"Teaching Device for Reducing Training Time," *Computers and Automation*, May 1960.

"Teaching Machine," *The New York Times*, October 11, 1960.

"The Teaching Machine," *Education Summary*, March 27, 1960.

"The Teaching Machine," *Mechanical Engineering*, September 1961.

"Teaching Machine Experiment in Fire Training," *Fire Engineering*, January 1961.

"Teaching Machines," *Bulletin of the Florida State Teachers Association*, June 1961.

"Teaching Machines," *The Indiana Teacher*, November 1960.

"Teaching Machines," *Journal of Business Education*, January 1961.

"Teaching Machines," *Kentucky School Journal*, November 1961.

"The Teaching Machines," *Time*, November 7, 1960.

"Teaching Machines Ahead of Methods," *Chemical and Engineering News*, December 4, 1961.

"Teaching Machines and Programmed Learning: Roster of Organizations," *Computers and Automation*, June 1961.

"Teaching Machines and Texts," *Kansas Teacher*, November 1960.

"Teaching Machines Permeate Convention Sessions," *Audiovisual Instruction*, June 1961.

"Teaching Machines: Sooner or Later Their Growth Will Be Translated into Profits," *Barron's*, October 30, 1961.

"Teaching Machines Take Hold in Schools and Industry," *Electronics International*, October 1961.

"Teaching Revolution: How Programed Learning Is Being Used to Instruct Employees in Major Industry," *Employee Relations Bulletin*, November 8, 1961.

"Tireless Tutor" (in "The Talk of the Town"), *The New Yorker*, February 13, 1960.

Tonne, H. A., "Ubiquitous Teaching Machine," *Journal of Business Education*, February 1961.

"Use of Teaching Machine Idea Bids Fair to Revolutionize Job Training," *Advanced Management*, July-August 1961.

Vander Meer, A. W., "Fear of the Newer Media," *ALA Bulletin*, October 1961.

Waller, Theodore, "Teaching Machines and School Libraries," *Library Journal*, April 15, 1961.

Weaver, David O., "Suggested Techniques in Preparing Programed Learning," *Journal of the American Society of Training Directors*, May 1961.

Weisenberg, Charles M., "Teaching Machines," *The Commonweal*, January 27, 1961.

———, "Teaching Machines—Bane or Blessing?" *Air Force*, March 1961.

West, L. J., "Teaching Machines: New Classroom Aids," *Southern Illinois Business Bulletin*, Summer 1960.

"What About Teaching Machines?" *Office Executive's Bulletin*, February 10, 1961.

"What Is the Potential of Audiovisual Devices?" *Audiovisual Instruction*, June 1961.

"What's New in Training? Teaching Machines, of Course," *For Line and Staff Supervisors*, October 30, 1961.

Wigren, Harold E., "Media for Tomorrow's Schools," *Educational Leadership*, May 1960.

"Will Teaching Machines Revolutionize Education?" *Michigan Education Journal*, December 1, 1960.

Winebrenner, D. K., "Launderettes and Learn-o-Mats," *School Arts*, May 1961.

———, "Teaching Machines: Practical and Probable," *The Nation's Schools*, August 1960.

Wittich, Walter A., "New Key to Learning: The Mechanized Tutor," *College and University Business*, February 1961.

Young, Jay A., "Programmed Instruction in Chemistry," *Journal of Chemical Education*, September 1961.

Young, Lewis H., "The Coming Boom in Teaching Machines," *The Home Study Review*, Summer 1960.

Zeaman, David, "Teaching Machines," *Grade Teacher*, September 1960.

Bibliographies

AID, June, July, October 1961, *et. seq.*

Campbell, Ina, *Teaching Machines and Programed Learning: A Bibliography*, Teaching Materials Corporation, New York City, 1961.

Fry, Edward B., Glenn L. Bryan, and Joseph W. Rigney, "Teaching Machines: An Annotated Bibliography," *AV Communication Review*, Vol. 8, No. 2, Supp. 1, National Education Association, Department of Audio-Visual Instruction, Washington, D. C., 1960.

Lange, Phil, *Materials on Teaching Machines and Programmed Instruction*, Teachers College, Columbia University, New York City. (Very short, but contains information on films which are commercially available.)

Leavitt, Jerome E., and Rilla J. Edgar, *Programed Learning and Teaching Machines*, Instructional Services Section, State Department of Education, Salem, Oregon, June 1961.

Lumsdaine, A. A., and Robert Glaser (editors), *Teaching Machines and Programmed Learning: A Source Book*, Department of Audio-Visual Instruction, National Education Association, Washington, D. C., 1960. (Contains a lengthy annotated compilation of published and unpublished papers as well as a bibliography.)

Lysaught, Jerome P. (editor), *Programmed Learning: Evolving Principles and Industrial Applications*, The Foundation for Research on Human Behavior, Ann Arbor, Michigan, 1961. (Contains a list of unpublished papers.)

Teaching Machines—Bibliography #52, Education Library, College of Education, University of Florida, Gainesville, Florida, November 1960.

Teaching Machines—Selected References, American Management Association, New York City, November 1961.